# GUERRILLA MILLIONAIRE

# GUERRILLA MILLIONAIRE

## Unlock the Secrets of the Self-Made Millionaire

### By Douglas Vermeeren
#### with Jay Conrad Levinson

 iUniverse®

GUERRILLA MILLIONAIRE
UNLOCK THE SECRETS OF THE SELF-MADE MILLIONAIRE

iUniverse books may be ordered through booksellers or by contacting:

iUniverse
1663 Liberty Drive
Bloomington, IN 47403
www.iuniverse.com
1-800-Authors (1-800-288-4677)

Because of the dynamic nature of the Internet, any web addresses or links contained in this book may have changed since publication and may no longer be valid. The views expressed in this work are solely those of the author and do not necessarily reflect the views of the publisher, and the publisher hereby disclaims any responsibility for them.

Any people depicted in stock imagery provided by Thinkstock are models, and such images are being used for illustrative purposes only. Certain stock imagery © Thinkstock.

ISBN: 978-1-4917-7387-1 (sc)
ISBN: 978-1-4917-7389-5 (hc)
ISBN: 978-1-4917-7388-8 (e)

Print information available on the last page.

iUniverse rev. date: 8/14/2015

# Contents

## PART 2—MONEY AND HOW YOU CAN JOIN THE MILLIONAIRES CLUB

## PART 3—WHAT WILL YOU DO TO START THE BALL ROLLING?

# Foreword by Jay Conrad Levinson

IN ORDER FOR YOU to become an authentic self-made guerrilla millionaire, it makes a whole lot of sense for you to learn from one. That's exactly what you're about to do as you open the pages of *Guerrilla Millionaire* by Douglas Vermeeren, with an enthusiastic assist from me.

Yes, the book is loaded with inspiration, but that's not why you're going to love it. It's also loaded with information, and that's why you're going to love it even more.

It takes you by the hand and leads you from your current financial situation, whatever it may be right now, to joyful abundance—a blessed state if ever there was one. And there is. Doug and I have done our best to take you right to it and help you feel at home there.

For that to happen, you'll need some plain talking and a chunk of practical, real-life advice that has worked for Doug and myself, for others, and that can work for you.

This isn't the kind of advice you'll find in most other books devoted to increasing your wealth. But it's the kind you must have if you're going to give wings to your dreams—our plans for you in this book.

Fasten your seat belts because we're going to spill all the beans, reveal all the secrets and not hold back for one moment.

You're going to understand truths about wealth and money that the vast majority of people never learn. You'll discover what money can and can't do, and why money is not the only key to happiness, but a definite help in opening the door to freedom and opportunity. You'll also discover that learning and implementing the tiny habits of the wealthy can result in your accumulating a large fortune.

Wise people have said that it's better to know some things about your spouse than everything about marriage. They also point out that it's better to know some things about becoming a millionaire than everything about money.

Those things are coming up in the following pages. This is not a complicated book. It's a simple, straightforward book for people who want simple, straightforward guidance toward achieving what others merely dream about.

Now, get ready for that dream to become true.

Jay Conrad Levinson
DeBary, Florida

# Preface

THERE ARE HUNDREDS, if not thousands, of books on creating wealth and becoming rich, so why do we all need another one? What makes this one unique and different? Well, if you are like me you've looked at a lot of the other books and they are either too simplistic and don't provide any practical insights into becoming wealthy, or they are just too complex for the average person to benefit from. You'd need a degree in economics just to get through the table of contents. I searched everywhere for a book that could provide clear, practical and applicable insights that would work. And I didn't find one, so here we are.

So what qualifies me to write such a book? Most people know me for my research into the lives of more than 400 of the world's top achievers. This is the same kind of research that Napoleon Hill did when he created his landmark book, *Think and Grow Rich*. The major difference between Hill's work and my own is that he studied innovators and inventors and specifically looked at what they did—their behavior. Now here we are one hundred years later, and a lot has changed. My research included business models and wealth categories that did not exist in his day. For example, I included multinational corporations, network marketing, Internet business models, celebrities and athletes—all categories that either didn't exist in the early 1900s or were not really making the kinds of dollars that they are today. I found a lot of things to support Hill's findings, success really can grow from powerful personal beliefs. But I also found a lot of information that was unavailable in Hill's day, especially in the area of thought. Brain science is still a very new field.

From the research that I conducted over the last several decades have come several books and other projects that have helped to create great success for individuals all over the world. (One such project is another Guerrilla book that I highly recommend as a companion to this one—*Guerrilla Achiever* by Jay Conrad Levinson and Douglas Vermeeren.)

Needless to say, as I have presented the success strategies from my studies of the world's top achievers, I have often been asked a very direct question: "While achievements are great, what we really want to learn is how to make more money. How do the top achievers do it?"

This is a very valid question considering that the vast majority of the top achievers involved in my research were self-made millionaires and billionaires. They had achieved incredible growth when it came to finance and abundance in their lives. My research uncovered many of their strategies, and these strategies were unique and very different from what most financial planners were telling the general public.

In fact, much of what I found was different from what many of the financial teachers of the day were sharing. It was almost like they were getting their information from books that were written a hundred years ago. It doesn't take a lot of observation to notice that we live in a much different world today. Lessons on how to become a millionaire in 1911 are often missing a few of the details required for today.

With this question of building wealth at the forefront, I set up to review my research and conduct some additional searching to find out what makes wealth today.

Now here's where the exciting part comes. As soon as I began to look at the research, I began to see patterns emerge. Patterns on how the rich made money, spent money and even thought about money.

Naturally, I wanted to know how valid my findings were, and so I put these lessons to the test first in my own life. And they worked. In my first six months I was able to create a small fortune of $1.6 million. These mysterious lessons worked! And they worked quickly!

I'm an average guy, I did not come from a background of wealth. One of the most valuable lessons I discovered was that all the attributes that made a person wealthy could be learned and put into practice by anyone.

As demand grew to learn the secrets I had found, I decided to formalize them into a learning program called Millionaire Training Systems. This program utilizes the expertise of many of the top achievers I had originally studied, but I also found several new people who understood and practiced these lessons. This program has been in operation since 2008 and has seen great success on nearly every continent on the globe. Many of these lessons are shared in this book.

As we begin, I want to share just a few thoughts about this book. First, the title. Why did I choose to use the word *millionaire*? There are lots of books about wealth; why didn't I use the word *rich* or *wealth*? Why the word *millionaire*? This choice was specific and intentional. Let me relate an experience.

About a year ago, I was teaching a wealth seminar in Las Vegas. Before the event began I was approached by a gentleman who told me he had wanted to become rich for a long time, but had always struggled with the idea. I probed a little deeper and asked him what his definition of rich was.

He shrugged and just said, "To be comfortable, I guess."

I probed deeper again. "What does comfortable look like for you?"

He shrugged again. "I dunno. I suppose to not have to worry about money."

Again, I probed. "And how much would that take?"

This time, no shrug, just a worried look coming over his face. "I dunno. I never thought about it before."

If you can't identify the target you can never hit it.

In order to arrive at a destination you need to be able to identify it. Rule number one: a goal that is specific and clear becomes attainable and near.

That's why I included the word 'millionaire' in the title. It is specific and clear. You will know when you've hit it, and you will know when you are en route to get there. We will talk a little bit more about this later on—just know that a million is the destination.

## A NOTE ABOUT THIS BOOK

Oftentimes when people are reading books and the books include exercises, activities and questions, readers skim over them and don't give them a lot of attention. I caution you—DON'T DO THAT WITH THIS BOOK. This is a Guerrilla book, and if you've read one before I don't have to remind you that these books are different. We are not writing for passive readers.

In order for the information in this book to make a change in your life, it needs to become part of your life.

There are three kinds of learning:

1. Emotive learning. Emotive learning happens when you are inspired by a nice story or touching example, something that gives you warm fuzzies and makes you feel good. It can be motivating and get you thinking a little differently. There will be some of those stories in this book, but those things can only get you so far.

2. Procedural learning. This is the kind of learning you do when you watch a cooking show. These situations share a lot of how-to, but oftentimes when you encounter a new situation or see something that you haven't seen before, you are stuck. You've been trained a certain way, and you need specific circumstances to succeed. (By the way, this is why most financial planners don't work extremely well for most people—they have only a limited number of cookie-cutter solutions or products based on what their head office feels most people need. The products they offer are usually de-signed heavily in the companies' favor.) Some procedural learning is good, but if you can't make it personal, reject it. We will share some procedural learning in this book too.

But the most important kind of learning is this:

3. Implemented learning. This is the kind of learning where you actually implement and personalize the things you are learning to what is happening in your life right now. This is where your most powerful learning takes place and results actually begin to flow into your life. Most importantly, this is where you change and grow into the thing that you most desire—a better version of yourself.

This book has been designed with exercises, activities and questions to allow you to take advantage of all three levels of learning. I can promise you that if you take the time to let this book guide you through each of these kinds of learning, you will experience a change in your financial life.

So let's get started …

Douglas Vermeeren
Nassau, Bahamas February 2013

# PART 1

## Millionaires and Why You Want to be One

# Abundance, Wealth and Why You Want to Become a Millionaire

THE PHRASE "HOW TO MAKE MONEY" is one of the most-searched concepts on the Google search engine. There are more than 167 million results that claim to share effective advice for creating increased cash flow.

It is obvious that having more money occupies the minds of most people on the planet. And rightly so—you can't do much without having to pay for it. Your food, clothing, shelter, transportation and quality of life are all directly attached to your level of income.

Money has a significant impact on our entire day-to-day experience. Zig Ziglar once observed, "Some people don't think money is very important, but I think it ranks right up there with oxygen." You really can't get very far without it.

> *Money is for making things happen.*
> —Richard Branson

## IS MONEY HAPPINESS?

You've probably heard the statement that money never was happiness, but how closely are the two connected? Does money actually create more happiness? Does money actually change a person's situation? Does it actually make your life better? To answer this question we must first look at another important philosophical question: what is happiness?

Happiness has been described as a choice. We choose to be happy. Our happiness is very closely connected to our ability to make choices. Happiness comes from having more freedom and opportunity to make better choices. When you have the freedom and opportunity to explore your greatest potential, you experience the greatest happiness.

With increased freedom and opportunity, you can also benefit the lives of others around you. Great happiness also comes from blessing the lives of others. Money often opens the door to more freedom of choice and opportunity to explore. Therefore, it is reasonable to say that money contributes to happiness. Maybe this idea could be best expressed in the following equation:

*Happiness = Freedom and opportunity to explore*
*our potential and greatest desires*
*Money has the potential to expand freedom and opportunity*
*Therefore, money can contribute to happiness.*

So if happiness is enhanced by having an abundance of choice, it is safe to say that money can expand that. When financial abundance grows, so does our capacity to be happy.

*Wealth is the ability to fully experience life.*
—Henry David Thoreau

The less financial power you have, the less power you have to make choices. As a result, you become less happy.

Findings by the Institute of Economic Affairs show that happiness levels correlate directly with the amount of wealth a person accumulates, and they do not level off when assets reach a specific threshold, as some have thought.[1]

To prove the point, let's look at the opposite of wealth for a moment. When a person is poor, how much opportunity and freedom do they have? Are they happy about their situation? How do *you* feel when you don't have enough money to meet your obligations? What opportunities become closed to you when you can't afford the admission price? How free are you when you don't have enough money to pay your rent or utilities? How happy are you when you are burdened by a negative credit rating? I have yet to meet anyone who would be overjoyed to get a call from a collection agency.

Poverty does not provide peace of mind or happiness. Instead it creates a level of stress that affects sleeping patterns, appetites, energy levels and ultimately health.

> *When you are poor you have no choice but to cry over*
> *spilt milk because that was the last of it.*
> —Wendell Austin Payne

Poverty never was happiness. Statistical research demonstrates that frustration in marital relationships, particularly those that end in divorce, can often be traced directly back to financial woes.

The top three reasons for divorce in the United States are traced back to financial problems. Number one in this list is particularly interesting. The number one cause of divorce in the United States is called *financial infidelity*. Financial infidelity occurs when marriage partners spend their joint resources without consulting or considering the needs of the partnership. Naturally, this creates incredible stress in the relationship. When there is no money, the love soon dies. According to a report from MSN News, out of 300 interviewed divorce lawyers, the majority indicate that divorce is a result of financial infidelity more often than sexual infidelity.[2]

> *The greatest of evils and the worst of crimes is poverty …*
> *Our first duty—a duty to which every other consideration*
> *should be sacrificed, is not to be poor.*
> —George Bernard Shaw

When there is financial trouble people begin to act in ways that they otherwise would not. They are more likely to be unkind, uncaring and callous. Without money the brain operates in a reactive survival mode and everything in its path can become a potential threat.

Money affects more than just the happiness and circumstances of an individual. It affects the entire community of that individual.

While it may be said that the love of money is the root of all evil, it is more true to say that a lack of money is the root of all evil.

Research on crime in the United States confirms that areas of low income, low employment and high debt are areas of high crime. These low income areas have greater levels of depression, self-esteem issues, suicide, drug use and violent crime. The same cannot be said of higher income areas. In fact, this same study confirmed that 53% of individuals in prisons in the United States come from high poverty situations, with incomes of less than $10 thousand annually.[3]

*Lack of money is the root of all evil.*
—George Bernard Shaw

## DOES MONEY GUARANTEE HAPPINESS?

A recent study looked at this question in a unique way. This study found that money doesn't always equate with happiness. In fact, it really came down to what the person purchased with their money. Happiness is tied closely to spending habits. The study determined that purchases that provided a life experience often provided higher levels of satisfaction than the purchase of material objects.[4]

Experiences are what create our memories. Ronald Reagan, the fortieth president of the United States made this observation about money and memories: "Money can't buy happiness, but it will get you a better class of memories."

Money affects the memories we have of our childhood, teenage years and even our adulthood. No doubt your memories of these things affect not only the happiness with which you look back at your youth, but also how you want your financial circumstances to look today in order for you to be happy.

*The only question with wealth is what you will do with it.*
—John D. Rockefeller

A further study involving purchasing power and happiness looked at two extremes.[5] The first group in the study was made up of people who acquired wealth and spent it on expanding and enriching activities. The second group of people acquired wealth and spent it on fleeting fancies and items that did not return value. On the frivolous spending side there were even a few cases that included individuals who ended up with drug addictions, gambling issues and other forms of addictive behavior. Naturally, the happiness of both of these groups who had money was significantly different.

*Money can't buy you happiness, but it can buy you a*
*yacht big enough to pull up right alongside it.*
—David Lee Roth

Having money alone doesn't guarantee happiness. But how you spend it can. Spending choices are tied directly back to the concepts of freedom and opportunity. Some purchases will expand freedom and opportunity, while others will take it away.

## ARE RICH PEOPLE JERKS?

It has been supposed by some that when people become rich they become jerks—disagreeable, ornery, selfish and Scrooge-like. This is false. Money is the great magnifying glass. In some ways it is also a mirror that reveals true character.

If you were a jerk before, money will give you more power to become a bigger jerk. But if you were a kindhearted person before making your money, the money will allow you to be more of the same.

*All things the same—most people are happier on payday!*
—Anonymous

Hopefully by now you have been convinced that it is better to be wealthy than poor. Hopefully you have also been convinced that how you spend your wealth will determine your happiness with wealth. Wallace D. Wattles, the author of *The Science of Getting Rich*, stated that wealth was an essential component of success. He said: "Whatever may be said in praise of poverty, the fact remains, it is impossible to enjoy a complete and successful life unless one is rich." Let's find out how wealth would affect your experience.

## $1 MILLION TO SPEND!

Consider for a moment that I were to write you a check for $1 million. Take a moment and seriously think about what you would do with that money today. Make a list of ten things that you would do. Remember that to be successful with the training in this book, it is important to actually complete the exercises. Take sixty seconds and I do mean literally sixty seconds. I don't want you to spend too much time thinking about it. Shoot straight from the hip. What would you do with $1 million? Set your stopwatch and get writing!

1.
2.
3.
4.
5.
6.
7.
8.
9.
10.

What did you decide you wanted to buy?

What did you want to have?

What did you want to do?

What did you decide to spend the money on?

Typically a person spends their money on one of three things. How did your decisions fit into the three following categories?

Quality of life (Q)—The first category that most people spend their money on is in increasing their quality of life. This can include having less stress, more free time, the ability to eat the things they want, visit the places they want, wear the clothes they want, drive the cars they want, live in the house they want and so forth. Quality of life is directly connected to happiness. When we use our wealth to increase our quality of life we grow in our happiness.

Create (C)—This category is about creating things. Perhaps you want to create a business from an idea that you have had for a long time, or maybe you want to develop a project that you've been dreaming about. Often this category is about expanding something that is either going on in your life already or creating something new that you have always wanted to do. For example, one of the people in my coaching program has always wanted to record a CD of her own music. With an increase in wealth she has now begun her project.

Contribute (C)—When people have a level of financial abundance established in their lives one of the greatest sources of joy comes from helping others. That is exactly what this category is about. When you have reached a level of surplus in your finances you may be looking to contribute back to your community and the society around you. Again, an example from our coaching program: We have several individuals whose goal is once they have provided for their own financial needs to contribute back to feeding the needy, church missionary programs, helping provide supplies for schools in third world countries and even wheelchairs for those in need. Contribution is a significant activity that wealth allows you to participate in. A 2006 study in the Journal of Science found that giving away money always brings feelings of joy.[6]

In the future we will abbreviate these three factors as Q C C. (Quality of life, Create and Contribute.) We will refer to these often along the way.

## WHAT IS WEALTH?

We have talked quite a bit so far about the need for wealth and why you want to have it, but what is wealth? One author suggested that wealth is measured by how long you could maintain your current lifestyle without taking another paycheck. If you could only last a week or two weeks you don't have a lot of wealth. I like what oil-billionaire J. Paul Getty once said about money, "If you can still count it, you aren't rich."

The word wealth comes from a middle English word that actually means abundance. What does abundance mean? Abundance means overflowing. When your financial situation is overflowing then you have wealth. Perhaps it's for this reason, (and I will get into more detail on this in the following chapter as we discuss definitions of what a millionaire is) that I don't believe wealth is a specific amount as much as I believe it is a constant flow. Wealth is a constant overflowing of financial power to you, not a single event.

This can be well illustrated by individuals who win the lottery. That one-time win very seldom makes them wealthy in the long run. There is no constant flow of financial power toward them. In fact, there have been scores of studies that have demonstrated that most lottery winners are either where they were before winning or worse off in less than three years.

A regular recurring flow of abundance toward you will make you wealthy.

## BROKE OR POOR? WHAT'S THE DIFFERENCE?

As we begin our journey together to explore tactics and strategies that self-made millionaires use to create fortunes, there is a question that we need to answer to determine how effective the materials in this book will be for you. Are you broke or are you poor?

Your first thought might be to ask, what's the difference? Aren't they the same thing? Nope. Let's look a little more closely.

*Broke* means that you are temporarily in a tight spot. For the moment, your wallet is empty. Sometimes this can happen when you get surprised by expenses or setbacks that you didn't see coming. But even though things are tight, you are not in despair, you know things will change. Even rich people can end up broke from time to time. Broke is never permanent.

*Poor* is a state of mind. If you are poor, it doesn't matter what is going on around you whether good or bad, you will stay poor. You are in a state of despair and you can't see any hope for change. You don't take risks, because you believe they will never pay off.

If you are temporarily broke and are ready for a change, and believe it can happen, then this book is going to help—a lot. Broke can be fixed.

If you are poor, no book or program can help you until your thinking changes. Make the decision now that you want to be wealthy, that you can be wealthy and will be wealthy. Decision is the first step to change.

If you are poor, let's take a minute and look at why. A *"poor"* state of mind comes from habit. You have fallen into a poor state of mind because what you have been trying to do up until now has not yielded stellar results. As a consequence of experiencing repetitive failures, you have come to expect that you deserve the results you have had previously or you believe that your current results are your only possibility. You don't know what else to try and therefore believe that you have tried everything. You have grown comfortable living with less than you deserve.

*Change is possible in any financial situation.* Generally speaking, the only way something doesn't change is if a person continues doing what they have always done. Right now you are operating from what you currently understand.

The Chinese philosopher Confucius once described how to attain wisdom. He suggested that there were three ways:

Reflection (the most noble way)
Imitation (the easiest way)
Experience (the most painful way)

You've already tried experience, which got you where you are today.

Reflection generally doesn't help much either. Mostly because it is hard to rise higher than the thoughts with which you currently have to work. You can't expand beyond that which you have not yet understood.

But imitation ... Well, that's where we can help.

In this book I am going to share several time-tested strategies and formulas that have been used by multiple self-made millionaires before you. In my personal research, I have explored more than 1000 successful self-made millionaires and what they do differently from the rest of us. It is time for a change, and change is possible.

Poor thinkers, take a minute and think on this:

What is holding you back in your current financial circumstance?
What could you observe or learn that would allow you to create a different outcome?

My challenge to you is to go out and find someone to imitate who has already made it through what's currently holding you back. Pay careful attention to what they did to break through. It may surprise you to learn that not everything came easily to them either. Wealth requires perseverance and focused effort. But it can be done, and you've got to start thinking that way.

If you have not yet set a goal to be financially abundant, now is the time to do so. Wealth, not poverty, will allow you to begin to live the life you want and deserve.

## EXERCISES

Remember the power in this book will come into your life only as you apply what you are learning. The exercises are designed to help you make those changes. It will be well worth your while to pause and complete the exercises before moving on.

1. Make a list of the frustrations you are experiencing because of a lack of financial abundance in your life right now. After making the list, write how you will feel when these concerns are resolved and no longer require your attention. Notice your feelings in this exercise, as they will become strong motivators in future exercises.

2. Create a vision board that illustrates the freedoms and opportunities you will pursue as you grow your wealth. Your vision board should be a collection of images and photographs that reflect things you want to achieve or attain in your life. The easiest way to create this is to take a sheet of poster paper and then cut photos out of magazines that resonate with you as things you would like to have as part of your life. Be sure to put your vision board in a location where it can be seen daily as a reminder.

3. Make a commitment that you will look at your situation with a hopeful attitude rather than a poor spirit of doubt. If you struggle with feelings of disbelief, make a reminder card to keep your thinking on track. Remember that every problem you face to become a millionaire has been solved at one time by someone else. You can do the same.

There is no such thing as a problem. Everything is a puzzle, and there are solutions to puzzles. (This is a big challenge for many people. If this is also a challenge for you please check out the other

Guerrilla book by Jay Conrad Levinson and Douglas Vermeeren—
*Guerrilla Achiever.* It contains many great tools for turning your
thinking around and getting on track with your goals, especially
your financial ones.)

## QUESTIONS

1. What opportunities are you missing because of a lack of
   finances?
2. How does this make you feel?
3. What freedoms are unavailable to you because of a lack of
   finances?
4. How does this make you feel?
5. How would your quality of life change if you had the finances to be comfortable?
6. What would you create if you had the finances you needed
   to explore your dreams?
7. What would you contribute to the lives of others if you had
   the finances to do so?
8. What difference would this make in their lives?
9. How would this make you feel?
10. Are you ready to become wealthy?
11. Are you poor or broke?
12. What are the beliefs that are keeping you broke?
13. How can you overcome these false beliefs?
14. Are you ready to begin to build your wealth?
15. What does a wealthy life look like to you?

# What is a Real Millionaire?

My BEST FRIEND, Jason, was nine and I was almost nine. We were both walking to school on a sunny spring morning when it happened. We could hardly believe it was true. Then Jason reached down and picked it up. We had found twenty-five dollars on the sidewalk. We had never seen so much money in our lives.

Obviously someone had lost it. It was a busy street and no one was in sight. There was no way we could identify the money's owner. We decided it was meant for us.

Our first thoughts were that if we shared the discovery with our parents they would make us save it. We quickly developed other plans.

We had never skipped school before, but with this incredible luck we decided we really didn't have a choice. We put school on the back burner and walked nearly two miles to the closest department store. Inside the store were all the toys, games, comic books and candy we could imagine. We had both been there before but this time was different. This time we had we had twenty-five dollars.

It didn't take long for us to collect some of our favorite things and make the purchases. We were excited to notice that even after buying almost everything we wanted we had change left over.

As we walked home with shopping bags on each arm, I felt like we hadn't a care in the world. Jason turned to me and said, "Now I know what's it's like to be a millionaire."

It was at that moment I decided that was exactly what I wanted to be.

Naturally, twenty-five dollars was a far distance from a million. But because we had never had so much money before it had the same effect. I had the same feeling occur in my life the first time I received a single check for $400 thousand. I felt like a millionaire even though the check was less than half a million dollars.

Oftentimes a feeling of wealth comes from just having a significant amount more than what you started with. While the title of this book is *Guerrilla Millionaire*, it is important to realize that you don't necessarily need a million dollars to feel abundant. Your feelings of abundance as described in the first chapter of this book really come down to how you spend your money, not necessarily how much you have.

I guess that's why I thought it was important to define what a millionaire is near the beginning of this book. It doesn't really take a million dollars to feel like a millionaire, and neither does it take a million dollars to be considered as having millionaire status by the standards of many financial organizations.

## WHAT IS A MILLIONAIRE?

Research from the University of Toronto by Dr. Jeffrey Rosenthal estimates that there are more than 10 million millionaires in the world today.[1] Each year that number grows by more than 200 thousand new millionaires. Essentially that means there are more than 547 new individuals joining the millionaire club each day. That's more than twenty-two per hour.

That's an incredible number to think about. And naturally, it's good news because that means that there is more than enough hope for nearly everyone who would like to become a millionaire. It is very possible.

But what are the criteria being used to determine millionaire status?

As I have conducted research on millionaires over the last decade, I have discovered a handful of different definitions of what a millionaire is. It seems that there are many disagreements as to what actually constitutes a millionaire. I used to think that it was cut and dried—if you had an income of over $1 million annually you were a millionaire. But it's not that simple, considering how a person is taxed, how assets are accumulated and valued, and how capital gains and portfolio values are taken into consideration.

However, with all the confusion around what a millionaire really is, I'd like to share the three most common definitions, then talk about each one of them and share which one I favor (which is also the one we will be using for the purposes of this book), and why I think the other ones shouldn't really count.

As a heads-up, I use the QCC formula (Quality of life, Create and Contribute) as a guide as to what kind of millionaire actually gets to live a real-life millionaire experience. See if you can decide which best passes the test.

### Asset Millionaire Status

An asset millionaire is someone who, on paper, can demonstrate a million dollars of net worth. The assets on this list can include property, investments, vehicles and even antiques and artwork. The significant benefit that an asset millionaire has is that this kind of strategy provides for a wide variety of diversification. While not all investment gurus advocate diversification, it continues to be one of the most recommended strategies for long-term security.

While assets appear to offer security, there are challenges. One of the biggest, that I learned about firsthand, is if you need liquid cash, building your wealth on assets alone can sometimes create hurdles, especially when it comes to either selling the asset or getting the full valuation that you anticipated. I'll give you two examples to think about.

The first deals with one of my first big assets. You may think it a bit juvenile, but I think it is an excellent example that really shares the point. Throughout my early and late teens I collected comic books. But not just any comic books. I collected vintage collectible comic books. In my collection I had some valuable books, including some of the very first editions of Spider-Man, Iron Man, the X-Men and the Incredible Hulk. According to industry guides, these books were valued at thousands of dollars.

In my mid-twenties I decided it was time to sell them. I could really have used the money. Now, these were the days just before eBay and forums where collectors could sell to peers. The only avenue I had to sell my books was through a retail comic book shop.

I remember that Saturday well. I packed all my comics into my little red Volkswagen Jetta and drove downtown. The man at the shop had sold me hundreds of comics over the years. This time I was the seller. As I brought all of my books to him he smiled as he went through the collection. He admitted that I had many exciting jewels in my collection. In my mind I was expecting that thousands of dollars were headed my way. To my surprise, when we concluded he made his offer—$1,200.

I was shocked. I thought I had several books that were worth at least $1,200 on their own.

The shop owner then explained a few things to me that are important lessons in the context of what we are talking about—assets.

Lesson 1: Assets are worth only what someone is willing to pay for them. They are not always worth what the market suggests they are.

Lesson 2: If the demand or a market's ability to buy is low, the asset will diminish in value to meet the demand of the buyers. You've probably heard this described as either the law of supply and demand or marketplace ability.

Lesson 3: Peer selling is better than business buying. In other words, selling to a motivated buyer who is buying out of passion is better than selling to what I call a business buyer. Business buyers are always buying with profit in mind, and they will never pay more than they expect could make them a profit. A passionate buyer will pay almost any asking price, especially if you are the only source of supply.

The second example I want to share happened in real estate. It didn't happen to me, it happened to my grandfather. In 1955, my grandparents bought the home that they raised all of their children—my father and aunts—in. My grandparents decided then that they would stay in that house even into their retirement years and when one of them passed away, whoever remained would sell it and move into an assisted living home.

A few years ago my grandmother passed away. There was my grandfather, left with the house and his plan to sell the property. The market value suggested that the home was worth approximately $380 thousand. So my grandpa had a realtor list the home in that price range.

Month after month went by with no sale. The primary reason was that nearby you could buy a brand new house in a lake community for almost the same price. That house was still under a builders warranty and it was a lake community. Very few people would choose my grandpa's house, built in the mid-1950s, over that kind of deal.

Yet here was my poor grandpa, wanting to get into a seniors' center and stuck without the income to do it. After trying to sell the property for a little over a year a risky solution appeared. My cousin had a breakup with his girlfriend and needed a place to stay. Naturally, he came to Grandpa. But my cousin didn't want to buy. Instead, he wanted to rent the place.

Without a lot of choices, my grandpa agreed and let my cousin move in. While I don't know the details of this situation, it has really created a challenge for my grandpa. What does he do when his grandson is late with the rent? He can't very easily just kick him out. My cousin has now been there a few years and I know my grandpa has bumped into a few challenges so far. At the time of this writing my cousin is still at my grandpa's, and he crosses his fingers for the rent every month. Not a great way to live your retirement years and a very valuable example for all to consider.

Yet many people build their entire future on the plan that they will accumulate real estate assets and then sell them at retirement time.

Another consideration to keep in mind is that the value of assets can also change. The change can be positive, and naturally that's what you are hoping for over time, but it can also be negative. During the recession we saw significant drops in real estate values, even as much as 80% in some markets. If it comes time to retire and we hit another recession, you could be in for a big surprise.

Most people believe that asset accumulation will provide the most secure kind of financial future. In addition to real estate, they spend their entire lives preparing for retirement by building an RRSP (Registered Retirement Savings Plan), mutual funds and other similar investment products to provide for their future. While there are benefits to these assets, a little research will demonstrate that oftentimes they barely beat inflation, and when you need to liquidate them there are often penalties—fees and taxes—that actually leave you with no end benefit.

There is a lengthy track record to observe that these instruments rarely pay off as well as people expect in the long run. Look at seniors everywhere, just like my grandpa, reaching retirement age. I have yet to see a senior proclaim financial independence upon retiring with these kinds of assets. Instead, they start looking more carefully for seniors' discounts.

Assets look good on paper. But if you've ever gone into a restaurant and tried to buy dinner by just flashing the manager your balance sheet, you know that doesn't work well. Many of the people in this category aren't experiencing a brilliant quality of life along the way because their assets are tied up in time terms that don't make the assets easy to access.

An asset millionaire status has its limitations. But just so you don't think I'm totally against assets I want to state clearly that they do have their place. I currently have a lot of my money tied up in asset accumulation and preservation. But that isn't the foundation for my wealth, and we will talk about that in a moment.[2]

## Liabilities Millionaire Status

How this idea ever became considered to confer millionaire status I'll never know.

Here's the definition: A person is given this millionaire status if they have the ability to borrow, or leverage themselves to, the amount of a million dollars. In other words, you don't have the million dollars, but if you had to get it you could, by borrowing. To me, this is ridiculous. I am not against the idea of borrowing funds in the right circumstances, but I am against calling your borrowed money millionaire status. It's not your money.

Leveraging wealth in this way can create significant problems. In fact, this is what we saw as the primary problem behind the recent recession in the United States. People en masse leveraged their credit far beyond their ability to service that debt. The result was the economic catastrophe that followed. Spending stopped, companies downsized and people lost jobs. Without money circulating, foreclosures resulted and people lost homes and possessions. All this was a result of people leveraging their finances beyond their ability to pay back their debts.

*Running into debt isn't so bad. It's running into creditors that hurts.*
—Unknown

A second part of this problem that we will talk about later on has to do with what people purchase on credit. For now, just keep in mind that some purchases have very little value to return for what they ultimately cost.

When you are stuck in a prison of debt, you can't grow or create anything in your life. Instead, everything begins to shrink and disappear. True wealth is defined as how long you could maintain your current lifestyle without receiving another pay check. If you are living your life on credit you are actually living in reverse. Your future income is gone before you arrive in the future.

The single strangest definition of millionaire that I have come across in this category comes from a company in Panama by the name of Thetabiz Offshore Services—A millionaire is an individual who *resides* in a household whose net worth or wealth exceeds one million units of currency.[3] According to this definition I don't even need to have claim on any money. I just have to *live* in a residence of someone with assets of a million. So if my daddy is rich, I am considered a millionaire. This is very bizarre to me.

By this definition, I was a millionaire a lot earlier than I used to believe. When I was fresh out of college I rented a room from a multi-millionaire friend of mine in his home in California. What a terrible definition!

A liabilities millionaire isn't really a millionaire at all. But borrowing money can have its place and we will talk about that later.

> *If you think nobody cares if you're alive, try missing a couple of car payments.*
> —Earl Wilson

> *When you get in debt you become a slave.*
> —Andrew Jackson

### Cash Flow Millionaire Status

A cash flow millionaire is the definition of millionaire that I prefer. Essentially, it is exactly what it sounds like. Your regular cash flow is equal to a minimum of one million dollars annually. I specifically include the word *annually*. If we were to disregard the time factor of annually, the term millionaire loses its relevance. Most people earn several million dollars in their lifetime. But this is not the definition we are looking for. In my books, a millionaire must have an income of over a million dollars annually. A cash flow millionaire passes this test.

The reason why cash flow is king is because cash flow is the only thing that will really change your life experience. Cash is required to pay your bills and to pay for the experiences that you wish to have.

*In God we trust; all others must pay cash.*
—American proverb

In the world we live in cash flow is a priority. Without cash flow we cannot experience the freedom to explore our greatest personal potential that we spoke about in Chapter 1. Only cash flow allows you to take advantage of opportunities. When something marvelous comes along, only cash flow will allow you to participate. Cash flow changes your life experience. Cash flow is what allows you to enjoy life.

Naturally, once your cash flow has you living the lifestyle that you are seeking, you can use the excess cash to grow assets.

*When I was young I thought that money was the most important thing in life; now that I am old I know that it is.*
—Oscar Wilde

To become a cash flow millionaire you need to make an average of $2,739 a day, which comes down to $114 an hour or $1.90 per minute. Of course, when you are making your millionaire-level income you won't generally begin by making those amounts daily, hourly or by the minute. But it's important you know those numbers. The reason I like to break down the required cash flow into these increments is for the following three reasons.

**Reason One**

Many people look at the number *1,000,000* and they see all the zeros and get worried. In fact, when they see the zeros, they focus on them and worry that they will have zero chance of getting to the goal of $1 million. Seeing the smaller, more attainable numbers gives hope and a starting point.

**Reason Two**

Seeing these smaller numbers gives you the ability to see where you are currently and how far you are from your goal. Once you know what you are currently making daily, hourly and by the minute, you can see how far you are from your goal of generating a million dollars annually. When you can see how far you are from your goal, you can begin to consider what you need to do to grow to that level of income. We will get into more detail on this concept when we talk about creating multiple streams of income.

## EXERCISE

Consider how much your current net income is annually. (How much you bring home after taxes and mandatory government deductions, union dues, insurance or anything else that comes off your check before you get it.) Include the full amount you get to keep and ALL income streams you currently have. Now divide that by 365, divide that result by 24, divide that result by 60 and insert your answers in the blanks below.

365 days = $_____
24 hours a day = $_____
60 minutes an hour + $_____

How do those numbers compare with a millionaire income?

**Reason Three**

One of the most significant factors that keeps people from growing their wealth is that they don't use their time effectively. Ultimately, when you achieve wealth you will not be trading time for money, but in the beginning how you use your time will be one of the main resources you have to grow your wealth. Later in this book we will spend time talking about millionaire habits. How you use your time in the present will be a big determining factor that decides if you will receive an abundance of time and money later.

Figure 2.1: Income comparison

|  | Your current income | A millionaire income | The difference |
|---|---|---|---|
| Daily |  | $2739 |  |
| Hourly |  | $114 |  |
| By the minute |  | $1.90 |  |

## EXERCISE

We looked at how your daily, hourly and by-the-minute income stacks up beside a millionaire income. Now let's look at the difference of what your time is currently worth. By understanding what your time is worth, it is my hope that you will recognize that your time has value and that you will decide to use it more carefully from here on in. Do not use a regular work day to calculate these values. Use the 24-hour clock so that you can see what your time, and I mean all of it, is really returning to you right now. We will talk about specific choices you may want to start making when we get to the section of this book that talks about millionaire habits. You can use the dollar amounts you calculated above. Simply insert them into the appropriate blanks.

**How much is your time worth?**

Daily $_____

Hourly $_____

By the minute $_____

Oftentimes when they perform this exercise, people in my seminars are startled to see how little they are actually getting paid. Most people realize that their income, on a 24-hour scale, is barely above minimum wage. If this is how you are feeling right now, don't be discouraged. We will soon talk about how this can change.

*Many people take no care of their money till they come nearly to the end of it and others do just the same with their time.*
—Johann Wolfgang von Goethe

Just out of interest, would you be curious to know the annual, daily, hourly and by-the-minute incomes of some of the world's better known millionaires and business leaders? All of these values are approximate and based on information available to the public through shareholder reports and as published in Forbes magazine. Again, these amounts are for 24 hours a day, seven days a week. These people are earning considerable amounts of money—even when they are asleep.[4]

Indra Nooyi—Chairman and CEO, PepsiC.

| | |
|---|---|
| Annually: | $18,600,400.00 |
| Daily: | $50,960.00 |
| Hourly: | $2,123.00 |
| By the minute: | $35.38 |

Alan Mulally—President and CEO, Ford Motors

| | |
|---|---|
| Annually: | $19,856,000.00 |
| Daily: | $54,400.00 |
| Hourly: | $2,266.66 |
| By the minute: | $37.77 |

Josef Ackerman—CEO, Deutsche Bank

| | |
|---|---|
| Annually: | $2,779,840.00 |
| Daily: | $7,616.00 |
| Hourly: | $317.33 |
| By the minute: | $5.28 |

Bernard Arnault—CEO, Louis Vuitton

| | |
|---|---|
| Annually: | $7,702,960.00 |
| Daily: | $21,104.00 |
| Hourly: | $879.33 |
| By the minute: | $14.65 |

Donald Trump—CEO, Trump Organization

| | |
|---|---|
| Annually: | $73,000,000.00 |
| Daily: | $200,000.00 |
| Hourly: | $8,333.33 |
| By the minute: | $138.88 |

And just for fun:

Oprah Winfrey

| | |
|---|---|
| Annually: | $459,900,000.00 |
| Daily: | $1,260,000.00 |
| Hourly: | $52,500.00 |
| By the minute: | $875.00 |

## QCC MEASURES A REAL MILLIONAIRE

You'll remember earlier we talked about QCC (Quality of Life, Create and Contribute). QCC is very important when it comes to being a millionaire. This is the primary reason most people want wealth.

Sure, some people may say that they want it for security and to have a reasonable retirement fund. But if you think about it, those things are part of your quality of life. The only difference is that those people haven't expanded their quality of life ideas to include the present. How do you want your quality of life to be today, in the present? Only a cash flow millionaire has more opportunity to participate in these three areas today.

If you have set a goal to become a millionaire, then begin by deciding to be a cash flow millionaire and looking at what you can start doing to increase your daily, hourly and minute-by-minute average cash flow incomes.

> *Money is only a tool. It will take you wherever you*
> *wish, but it will not replace you as the driver.*
> —Ayn Rand

## QUESTIONS

1. What is a millionaire?
2. What is an asset millionaire?
3. What is a liabilities millionaire?
4. Does renting a room from a millionaire make you a millionaire?
5. What is a cash flow millionaire?
6. What is the best kind of millionaire to be? Why?
7. What kind of millionaire will you be?
8. Why is it beneficial to set daily, hourly and by-the-minute goals to become a millionaire?
9. How much could you possibly make daily with your current income stream?
10. Are there limits?
11. How can you expand your daily income, hourly income and minute-by-minute income?

# What are Your Chances
# of Making a Million?

THE GOAL OF BECOMING A MILLIONAIRE or becoming wealthy is probably one of the most common goals that people have. The idea of being able to meet this goal becomes a big quest for many people. In order to achieve the goal of becoming rich you have got to believe it is possible. Do you believe that it's possible for you to become a millionaire? If you don't believe it, you're finished even before you get started.

If you do believe, it is possible you have a head start over many people who have that same goal. But believing it is not enough. In order to become a millionaire you must have a strategy and a plan that will work. And even with those things in place, it will take a lot of hard work and determination.

Most people don't understand what is required to become a millionaire, other than the amount of money needed. Without a clear understanding of what is required, they make up a lot of obstacles in their mind that don't even exist.

You'll remember what we said in the introduction about goals. A goal that is specific and clear becomes attainable and near. But a goal that is mysterious and secret is one that you'll never accomplish and soon forget.

In addition to having clarity about what you want, it is important to also recognize a few things that will need to be accomplished so that your brain can get working on solutions.

In reaching your goal of becoming a millionaire, or any goal for that matter, it is important to understand that goal setting is simply a matter of increasing the probability that the outcome you want will occur. In other words, there is no success or failure. Every action is a step in the right direction. And with every step in the right direction, the probability that you will achieve your goal increases.

This concept is even more important when it comes to creating wealth. Lasting wealth is not created in a single event. It is created in increments. In my seminars I use the example of a human heart. It does not pump blood once every six months to keep you alive. It pumps regularly and consistently. That is the same way wealth is created. Consistent, steady, small victories, one after another and regularly.

*Never before in the history of the world have so many people had the opportunity to be wealthy beyond their wildest dreams.*
—Tod Barnhart

In other words, if you want to have a million dollars, it's not going to be a straight course to the bank, where your million will be waiting for you. It will be a journey of increasing the probability that you will get that million. You do this by being the right person, doing the right things, surrounding yourself with the right opportunities, situations and people, and then acting on them consistently and regularly. The money will then arrive not in one lump sum, but in small amounts that together create a total sum of one million dollars or more. Things may not go smoothly every time, but as you do more of the right things, the probability of your success will increase. Naturally, the better you get at learning these strategies the more frequently the money will appear and the greater the amount will be also.

Aristotle once said, "That which is probable is most likely to occur." It may sound simplistic, but this is the way all goals are achieved. If you want to become a self-made millionaire, it will require making changes to your current lifestyle and activities. There is a reason that self-made millionaires are successful. They do specific things in a specific way, and that's what gets them the results they are seeking. As you come closer and closer to their pattern of living you will naturally see your wealth increase as well. This pattern of wealth is very important.

## PERSONALIZE, INNOVATE AND IMPROVE

By modelling the patterns that others have used to become self-made millionaires, you will increase your chances of being able to do the same. However, there is a danger. It is not enough to emulate what others have done. Times have changed and so must you. What others have done may provide great lessons to consider when you're starting out, but you need to personalize, innovate and improve on what they have done.

### Personalize

Personalizing the success of others is a crucial element of success. It gives you a starting point and some patterns to consider following. Personalizing successful thinking and actions will make them yours. In order to become wealthy, you must spend time thinking and planning. Action should support your best ideas.

A recent study determined that the average person has an average of six ideas each year that could be turned into a million-dollar enterprise. The challenge, I believe, is two things. First, most people don't do anything with the ideas they have. And second, maybe even more common, people rush into ideas they haven't taken the time to think through and implement properly. Remember that all massive ideas are a gift. In order to become effective you must take the time to create actions that will support your best ideas.

## A Note on Imitation

Imitation is dangerous. By imitating, you have immediately created competition for yourself. When imitating, you must find a way to separate yourself from this competition. This is done by taking the best you can observe and then personalizing that experience to become your very own.

An interesting little thought on personalizing success. To turn what you find into what you fund, you simply need to take out what "I" am doing and replace it with "U."

*FIND must become FUND if you are to be successful.*
*Be yourself—everyone else is taken.*

## Innovate and Improve

Let me use the example I spoke of in the introduction to this book. You want to become a self-made millionaire. What if I were to tell you everything you must do to become a millionaire, but I got my information from what it took to become a millionaire in 1911? How effective do you think you would be?

Naturally, there would be some great information, but most of it would be dated. The same is true when you are trying to pattern yourself after the self-made millionaires around you. You will have to innovate on what you learn to best suit your current circumstances. The world is always changing and improving and to be successful in it, you will have to innovate as well.

Hockey great Wayne Gretzky was once asked what made him such a great hockey player. His answer was, "I skate to where the puck is going." There is wisdom in this for wealth building also. The money is always made on the front edge of the wave of where things are going, not where they've been.

So where do you find out where things are going? The best information can be found in trade journals, magazines, reports and online news. If you are serious about becoming rich you should be delving into these resources.

*Innovation distinguishes between a leader and a follower.*
—Steve Jobs

So before we talk about how to increase your probability of building your wealth, let's take a look at where you are today. The following is a test based on the most common attributes, skills, habits and traits of self-made millionaires.

Go ahead and complete the test and then we'll compare your answers with other self-made millionaires. As we compare answers, I will share why some of these answers are important. Where necessary, you may want to make some changes in your life to increase your chances of becoming a self-made millionaire. Remember, the closer you can pattern your life after the examples of those who are millionaires already, the more likely your results will conform to match theirs.

**THE MILLIONAIRE TEST**

1.  In what country do you live?

    *Answer and explanation:* Why does it matter where you live? Well, some countries produce more millionaires more rapidly and with more ease than others. According to the World Wealth Report by Merrill Lynch, the top millionaire-producing countries (number of millionaires in parentheses) are:

    1.  United States (3,104,000)
    2.  Japan (1,739,000)
    3.  Germany (924,000)
    4.  China (535,000)
    5.  United Kingdom (454,000)

6. France (396,000)
7. Canada (282,000)
8. Switzerland (243,000)
9. Australia (193,000)
10. Italy (170,000)
11. Brazil (155,000)
12. India (153,000)

The results above don't take into consideration population sizes, nor do they account for the average incomes of the balance of the country. After those considerations have been taken into account the prime countries in which to become a millionaire are:

1. United States
2. Japan
3. Germany
4. United Kingdom
5. France
6. Canada

If you live in any of the six countries in the second list you can give yourself full points. If you don't live in one of these countries, it's not the end of the world. With the way that technology, specifically the Internet, is bringing the world together today, your chances of becoming a millionaire are increasing. Another consideration that the question of geography highlights is what country you ought to be doing more business in. Although I am Canadian, I do most of my business in the United States.

By the way, Los Angeles County in the United States has more millionaires than anywhere in the world, at 262,800 households with annual incomes of over $1 million.[1]

2. When were you born?

*Answer and explanations:* This is a bit of a trick question. Millionaires have been made in every age of the world. And wherever human needs exist you will find alongside that the possibility of becoming rich. However, if we look at the history of technology, innovation and invention have always facilitated the growth of wealth. So when is the best time to become a millionaire? Any time from here on. Start now.

Naturally, as technology has become more available to the masses, the number of millionaires has grown exponentially. Consider the following table.

Figure 3.1: Millionaires in North America

| Year | Number of millionaires in North America |
|------|------------------------------------------|
| 1750 | 1 |
| 1850 | 19 |
| 1890 | 4,000[a] |
| 1927 | 15,000[b] |
| 1978 | 450,000 |
| 1981 | 638,000 |
| 1988 | 1,500,000[c] |
| 2009 | 4,715,000[d] |

[a]The American Experience, PBS. Produced by Ric Burns. April 13, 1998.

[b]Business/Economy Report, 1920–30.com.; Tax Reports from the Treasury Department.

[c]Kevin Phillips, *The Politics of Rich and Poor,* see "Report on Income and Wealth Inequality," US Statistical report.

[d]"Countries with the Most Millionaires," *Bloomberg Businessweek.* population reference bureau.

The number of millionaires has increased with time. This is directly correlated to technology improvements that allow for businesses to reach out to more people. Therefore, the younger you are, the more chance you will have to adopt the most recent technology and thus increase your chances of becoming a self-made millionaire.

This rule of technology and wealth growing together is attached to one of my big pet peeves. I am pleased when I see some of today's younger generation so gifted at using technology. But I become a bit frustrated when I see that many of them use those gifts to play games, surf the Internet or text rather than create something of value.

3. For you, failure is …

    A. Unthinkable; not an option
    B. Most likely
    C. A common occurrence
    D. Part of the game

*Answers and explanations:* For Question 3 the best answer is *A.* Failure should be unthinkable. Losing is a state of resignation. Self-made millionaires do not look at problems in this way. Instead, they look at problems as puzzles and will not quit until they have found solutions to the puzzles they are facing. Many people who have taken this test in our seminars select *D.* However, I want to caution against this approach. Studies have shown that when you expect failure or loss to be a necessary component of success, you will experience more of it. Remember the old adage that you generally find whatever you are looking for. If you believe that something has to be difficult, you have a tendency to make it difficult. There is a term for this in psychology—investment bias. Essentially the theory of investment bias states that an individual will not accept a reward until they believe they have paid the appropriate price. Many people keep from having riches in their life because they feel they have not earned them. I find people who feel this way very interesting. They claim they haven't yet paid the price for success or wealth in their life, but in reality they have no idea of how much they do have to pay to be successful. Instead of finding out what it really takes to be successful, they assume that they know what is required of them. In reality there is no mathematical equation suggesting you need to put in X number of hours or X number of years before becoming wealthy. X number of failures is not required to create success.

5.  When you start a new project or task, what part do you like best?

   A.  The novelty at the beginning
   B.  The progress while I work
   C.  Finally finishing it

***Answer and explanations:*** For Question 4 the best answer is C. The only time you make money is when you complete a task. The biggest challenge that most unsuccessful entrepreneurs face is something called inaptitudinal reasoning. This is simply a fancy name for split focus. Too often entrepreneurs shift gears every time they get excited about a new idea. They put all their energies into every new idea, while their original ideas remain unfinished. In order to create ongoing cash flow, you need to complete what you start. You only get paid on a finished job.

4.  What do you do when you have a big decision to make?

   A.  Gather all the information possible
   B.  Follow my gut instincts.
   C.  Consult my friends, family and colleagues
   D.  Get advice from professionals and consultants

***Answer and explanations:*** For Question 5 the best answer is *B*. Your best answers need to be quick and instinctual. As you gain more experience in making quick decisions, your decisions will become better. Some people answer that *D* is the best option, but often professionals and consultants make their decisions from positions of fear. (Perhaps that is one reason why they tell entrepreneurs what do to and provide them services rather than become entrepreneurs themselves.) They are paid to protect entrepreneurs and get them out of trouble. If you begin with them on the starting line, you may never leave the starting line.

*I never get the accounts in before I start up a business.*
*It's done on a gut feeling, especially if I can see that*
*they are taking the mickey out of the consumer.*
—Richard Branson

As a side note, I was involved in a study once that researched where our biggest regrets come from. The answer: not following our gut instincts. Think about it. What is the thing that bothers you most from your past? I would be willing to bet it has something to do with a time when you knew in your gut what you should do but chose to do the opposite.

*Experience taught me a few things. One is to listen to your*
*gut, no matter how good something sounds on paper.*
—Donald Trump

5.  From the following statements, which are true in your case?

    I have affectionate parents.
    I have a supportive partner.
    I have a deep religious faith.

    A.  None of the above
    B.  One of the above
    C.  Two of the above
    D.  All of the above

*Answer and explanations:* For Question 6 the best answer is *D*. Having a secure support network can give you the confidence and courage required to pursue wealth. It is not an easy road and taking it alone can be dangerous. In *Think and Grow Rich*, Napoleon Hill points out that, generally speaking, men reach their most successful times after the age of forty. He speculates that this has a lot to do with finding stability in life with a supportive partner. Having a supportive partner of my own, I can testify that her presence makes a big difference for me.

5.  Think of how much you make in a year. What would you put more effort into: not losing a similar amount or getting the equivalent of three times that amount but risking the loss of everything?

    A.  Not losing the money
    B.  Getting the increase in money but risking its loss

*Answers and explanations:* For Question 7 the best answer is *B*. Yet it is important to clarify the word *risk* in this question. I am not talking about throwing a set of dice or taking a chance on the roulette wheel. That isn't risk. That's stupid.

The risk I am referring to is based on evaluation. The word *evaluate* means to place a value judgment on a specific matter. Before we participate in any opportunity we need to use our best judgment to evaluate its level of risk and security. Successful entrepreneurs do not proceed unless they are confident that the value significantly outweighs the risks.

Just a note on the other answer in this question—"Not losing the money." To focus on not losing what you already have excludes you from the possibility of gaining more. The old Indian proverb says it best: "The hand that holds too tightly onto yesterday cannot accept the gifts of tomorrow."

3.  If you achieve the great success you seek, you see yourself as a

    A.  Business owner
    B.  Famous person

C.  CEO of a company
D.  Valuable employee

*Answers and explanations:* For Question 8 the best answer is A. Business owners make up the vast majority of millionaires. I'll explain more as we go. Let's look at the other answers for a moment.

Valuable employees and CEOs of companies both have caps on what they can potentially earn. In the case of the CEO, the shareholders of the company have much to do with deciding the salaries they will allow to be paid to the company leadership.

There may be many famous people who make decent money, but many famous people are broke. Often, while famous people are a hot topic, many of them fail to structure their finances for the day when their fame will no longer carry them.

Statistics confirm that 84% of all self-made millionaires arrived there by owning their own business. A business owner has no cap on how much money they can make. They get to decide what their limits are or if there will be any limits at all.

5.  You are peacefully walking down the street, and suddenly, a flowerpot falls on your foot. Ouch! What is your reaction after saying "#@#%$^ᶜ&!" and recovering from the intense pain?

A.  That is bad luck. Why me?
B.  How lucky! It's a miracle it didn't land on my head.

*Answers and explanations:* For Question 9 the best answer is B. Wealthy individuals are optimistic. This does not mean that they are positive to the extent of being blind to real challenges and difficulties. It simply means that they look at making the best of everything that comes their way, rather than letting a negative situation paralyze them.

In other words, they don't stand still in moments of adversity to hold a pity party. They move through challenges as quickly as possible to create the next positive situation. Positive situations often always follow any negative occurrence.

3. You have been fired. What do you do with the severance money?

    A. Save it until you get a job
    B. Take a relaxing vacation to sort out your next plan
    C. Invest in a personal project
    D. Invest in stocks to increase it

*Answers and explanations:* For Question 10 the best answer is C. Ideally, your personal project is an event that you can control. You can make it successful, and the outcome can be highly financially beneficial. Similar to Question 8's answer, Question 10s C allows you to invest in your own business. As a business owner there is no limit to what you can do.

Investing in stocks might also be a good idea if you really know what you are doing. But for most people that is not the case.

Saving the money until you get another job doesn't really change your situation much, considering you were just fired from a job. It is very possible you could be fired again. Going from one job to another is like swinging from vine to vine in the jungle. You still have to swing to stay in motion and pay your bills. You aren't really creating any progress, just swinging from vine to vine.

And to use your severance money to take a vacation may give you a needed break, but you have done nothing to increase further cash flow. When the vacation ends, what then?

5. What can you say about your academic record?

    A. Excellent; I was always on top.
    B. Normal; I finished my studies.
    C. Mediocre; I tried but I couldn't.
    D. I left school so I could build a business.

*Answers and explanations:* For Question 11 the best answer is *C* or *D*.

Answer *A* is the most uncommon among millionaires. Not only do people who are highly educated spend more time in school, they spend less time making money in the real world. They also begin to adopt the thinking and habits of those with whom they surround themselves (i.e., students with big loans and professors who often make a meager teaching salary. For more on how those you surround yourself with affects your ability to become rich, check out my book *Network like a Millionaire*).

Many top business leaders and those in society who have created significant wealth left school to start a business or dedicate more time to a business they started while in school.

Bill Gates and Mark Zuckerberg are two excellent examples. While in school, Fred Smith, founder of Federal Express, was granted a C- on his business plan for FedEx. He has since gone on to turn FedEx into one of the world's leading shipping services. Statistics demonstrate that academe is not a great place to get support to grow billion-dollar ideas.

5. You planned a picnic to spend the day with family and friends. The day arrives, morning rises and it is pouring rain. What do you do?

   A. Find an inside activity
   B. Call everyone to reschedule
   C. Stick to the plan and have a picnic
   D. Ask for input from everyone on what they want to do instead

*Answers and explanations:* For Question 12 the best answer is *A*. If you have ever had an event cancelled and tried to ask everyone what they wanted to do, you know that you just can't get anywhere with that approach.

Wealthy and successful business leaders understand that

*they* must take a leadership role, and in order to succeed, *they* must set the course. Success is never found in trying to adopt the opinions of others.

*I don't know what the key to success is, but the key to failure is to try and please everyone.*
—Bill Cosby

If you chose to stick to the plan and still have the picnic in the rain you are also way off. In order to grow your wealth you have got to be able to avoid disasters when you see them coming. You must be aware and have the ability to adapt when necessary. If you planned to go down a road in your car and there was a semi-trailer truck coming directly at you, would you continue your course toward an accident just because that's the course you had originally set out to take? Of course not. You would readjust to either take a different route or wait until the truck was out of the way. Be smart.

Rescheduling isn't always necessary either. Too often when things are rescheduled and put off they never get accomplished.

The best answer is to find a new inside activity. If there is one thing I have learned from my research of the world's top achievers it is this: Top achievers are not perfectionists. They are improvisers. They wonder less about why something didn't work and spend more time figuring out how to make it work.

In my seminars I like to present this scenario when talking about this question to make my point clear. Imagine I had a check for you in my office for a million dollars and all you had to do to get it was pick it up today. How hard would you try to get there? Would rain keep you from coming? What if you were sick? Would you still make the journey? What if you had to drive for twelve hours? What about having to take a plane ride over? Would any of these things stop you?

Most answer that they would be there at almost any cost.

But in real life most people don't recognize that a solid

commitment like this is what is required. Casual commitment is the common excuse for the poor. The rich are innovators and masters at making things happen no matter what.

5.  If there was a million dollars cash for you on the other side of a field of explosive land mines, what would you do?

    A.  Stay put
    B.  Make a run for it and hope for the best
    C.  Go slow and steady
    D.  Follow someone who knows the safest route

*Answers and explanations:* For Question 13 the best answer is *D*. Staying put as suggested in answer *A* is what most people do in life. They stay exactly where they are, and as a result they think they will lose nothing. What they fail to realize is that the world around them is constantly changing. Even if they stay put they are automatically falling behind. You have to be moving forward to even keep up.

The second answer, of making a run for it and hoping for the best, may get quick results in the short term. But in the long run it does not create lasting success. Without a system to create lasting success, there can be no lasting wealth.

Slow and steady will yield some results, but it never creates opportunities for high levels of growth. The journey in this way takes too long and does not provide enough of a payoff.

Obviously the final option, *D*, is the best.

A mentor is someone who has been there before and understands potential obstacles and challenges. They also understand correct expectations. The most common challenge is that people have incorrect expectations about creating wealth. Often they don't understand what is required of them, how much time it will take or how much money they can make and so forth.

Having a mentor who has correct expectations can make

an incredible difference. Indeed it can make all the difference as to whether you will get to your million and how quickly it will happen.

After people understand they need a mentor, the most common question we get is, where can a person find a mentor? Not everyone knows a millionaire. And most people who do know a millionaire don't know one that has the time to become a mentor. So where will you find yours? If you are serious about acquiring a mentor who can help you on your journey to wealth, you would do well to look into our programs. We have been successful in helping create a real difference in our clients' finances and we can help you, too.

**How did You Do?**

If you didn't do brilliantly on the test, don't worry. The answers are not definite, and there are many exceptions to the answers given here. These answers are based on the highest percentages of self-made millionaires in the world today. If you did score high then you are right on track to growing more wealth in your life.

Ultimately the goal of this test is to get you thinking. Your thinking is ultimately what will allow you to change your situation. (We will talk more about this when we get to Chapter 6.) Hopefully you have noticed that self-made millionaires look at situations, especially challenging ones, a little differently.

> *There are enough needs available to facilitate*
> *everyone in the world becoming a millionaire.*
> —J. Paul Getty

As you begin to look at situations differently, your results will follow. Wealth comes to those who believe in themselves and are willing to trust their future to their best efforts. Everyone has the opportunity to become rich.

---

### INTERESTING SELF-MADE MILLIONAIRE STATISTICS AND FACTS:

- Most have been married to the same partner for over 28 years.
- Most have an average of three kids.
- 50% have wives who do not work outside the home.
- 32% are business owners.
- Most wake up between 6–7AM each day.
- 83% are not considered workaholics (they work less than 30 hours per week).
- Most spend an average of $41 thousand for a car.
- 61% have never received an inheritance or financial gift.
- 50% buy household supplies at warehouse stores (e.g., Sam's Club or Costco,
- 71% write a shopping list before grocery shopping.

*Source:* Compiled from questionnaire feedback received from attendees of the author's events.

---

## EXERCISES

Remember, the power in this book will only come into your life as you apply what you are learning. The exercises are designed to help you make those changes. It will be well worth your while to pause and complete the exercises before moving on.

1. Review the Millionaire Test regularly to explore how you can increase your probability of becoming a millionaire by bringing your answers into closer proximity of self-made millionaires.
2. Look at some of the statistics and facts about millionaires in this chapter, and see how you measure up. Even these little things will make a difference for you.

3.  Observe millionaires wherever you can find them: in real life, news reports, magazines and books, especially their biographies. Whatever you can find to observe their habits and traits will be useful. Look specifically for the attributes that are making them successful, and try to emulate those characteristics in your own life. Remember, you are seeking to increase probability by doing what they do. (Don't forget to innovate, personalize and improve.)

4.  Explore how you can personalize, innovate and improve the money building systems and strategies that you observe around you.

## QUESTIONS

1.  What role does increasing probability have in accomplishing any goal?

2.  What will you do to increase the probability of becoming a millionaire in the following areas:
    Geography—Where do you need to be—locally and on a larger scale—to make this happen better?
    Associations—Who do you need to spend more time with?
    Activities—What activities do you need to spend more time doing?

3.  Why do you need a mentor?

4.  Where will you find that mentor?

5.  What little changes can you make today that would bring your life closer to that of the average self-made millionaire?

# How are People Becoming
# Self-Made Millionaires Right Now?

**I AM NOT A COOK.** But every once in a while for fun I will try to make a birthday cake. As I have tried to make these occasional cakes, there is one thing I have been very thankful for and have found essential for my success. That one thing has been a recipe to follow.

The recipe gives you the guidance to see the creation of a cake from the very beginning through to the end. Without it, the mission to make a cake would most likely end in disaster.

Today there are many recipes to becoming a self-made millionaire. When they are followed, success is attainable. Some of these recipes are easier than others. Some of these recipes will be easier for you based on your specific skill sets, talents, interests and starting point.

In this chapter I will share some of the most common ways people are becoming self-made millionaires today.

I invite you to pay close attention to each of these significant areas. Think carefully about what ideas and strategies fit best with the direction you are heading in your life and how you can develop a plan to put yourself on a similar path.

Naturally, your chances of becoming a self-made millionaire are greater in the areas where the most millionaires are found. You'll remember our earlier discussion on increasing probability. I pointed out that when something becomes probable because you have put yourself in the right situation and surrounded yourself with the right people, places, things and education, the chances of a given event occurring in your life increases dramatically. So if you would like to increase the chances or probability that you will become a self-made millionaire, you would be best to align yourself with these methods that the majority of self-made millionaires are using to create their success.

Most millionaires today are made within one of the three major categories. I will further break these down to demonstrate more specific activity in each category, but these three major areas are Business and Entrepreneurship, Technology and Innovation and lastly, Investment. And yes, these are in order. Naturally, some of the self-made millionaires that we will look at combined and overlapped these categories. Doing that will increase your chances even more.

## BUSINESS AND ENTREPRENEURSHIP

Eighty-four percent of all self-made millionaires are made in the realm of business and entrepreneurship. Very few millionaires are made in salaried jobs or positions. The vast majority of self-made millionaires have given up a regular job and replaced it with a business of their own.

The most valuable aspect about owning your own business is that there is no limit to the growth of your income. You are the only one who will decide when you have a salary cap.

When choosing what business to pursue it is important to look at a few things.

### What Problem are You Solving?

The most money is found in solving the biggest and most relevant problems. If you are not providing any real or valuable solution to people they will not pay for your services. The greatest amount of wealth can be created by finding a significant problem that concerns a large group of people.

> *Problems are only opportunities in work clothes.*
> —Henry J. Kaiser

> *We are continually faced by great opportunities brilliantly disguised as insoluble problems.*
> —Lee Iacocca

## Repeat Business/Recurring Revenue

Business that repeats or recurs has many benefits. The most important is probably that you don't have to be constantly on the lookout for new customers.

One of the first businesses that I owned was an online casting directory for actors and actresses on the Internet. When I initially launched, I used a model that had me constantly running advertisements and meeting with new people daily. It took up a lot of time and cost a lot of money. When I expanded into other cities I found that I had a hard time just keeping up and keeping properly staffed. About two years into the business I changed my model from a one-time payment to a twelve month subscription that was paid monthly. I also required participants to opt out of the program on their own rather than me dropping them out at the end of their term. This is the same model that many fitness clubs use. I immediately noticed my profits rise, and burdens in staffing, advertising and my own personal time became far lighter.

> *A recurring revenue model is a great way to get paid again and again by your customer without having to hold out your hand and ask.*

Another significant benefit that I found was that my revenue stream became much more predictable. Initially, on the old program, I would begin a month not knowing what my profits would be for that month because they depended entirely on how many people responded to my ads and how many I could close when they came to see me. With contracts for monthly payments, I knew ahead of time within 10% what my profits would be. And with a clearer view of what the month looked like I could also begin to plan my own life better and even began to take time off.

Monthly membership programs are not the only way to generate recurring revenue. If you are offering a product through your business consider what other purchases may be valuable to your customer to encourage repeat business. In my Millionaire Money Masterminds there are several products that help people go deeper into their areas of interest. We have programs and training tools that take people deeper into learning about how to create wealth in real estate, build wealth in growing their business, increase wealth through relationships, negotiate deals better, find big and better deals, connect with high level people and so forth.

Many network marketing companies brilliantly use recurring revenue models in the form of auto-shipping products to your door every month.

I can't say enough positive things about creating a recurring, predictable revenue stream. It is the quickest way to make money while you sleep or are away on vacation. It is a very pleasant feeling to wake up and realize that during the night you made several thousand dollars, and you haven't even been in the shower yet.

## ROE

ROE stands for return on effort. You've probably heard of ROI, which is return on investment. Both are important. ROI is typically used to indicate a return on your money and is heard more frequently in the investment world. ROE focuses on your efforts and is heard more in the business world. Anyone who has been an entrepreneur for any period of time knows that a lot more goes into your business than money. A recent study suggests that the average entrepreneur spends more than 6sixty hours per week on their business.[1]

Productivity is not defined as doing more to get more. In fact, productivity is the gap between how much you do and how much you get. The wider the gap, the greater the productivity. The goal is to find ways to be more effective so that less of your efforts are required and your returns continue to go up. This can only be achieved by putting systems in place. We will talk more about systems later, but they are an essential part of increasing your ROE.

If you haven't yet started a business and feel that this is the route you would like to take to increased wealth, begin by evaluating carefully the effort that will be required versus the returns you will receive. Do not be afraid of hard work, just make sure that your only reward is not more work.

### Escape Route

Successful businesses always have escape routes. These can be found in either selling the business or simply diminishing your involvement in the day to day processes of the business. Great wealth cannot be accomplished when you are bogged down by the day-to-day details of your business. You need to be free to guide the business and explore opportunities to expand it. I often cringe when I hear people say that they "run" their own business. If your goal is to be wealthy then the goal isn't to run a business, it is to "lead" a business, much like the coach of a football team. The coach leads the team, he doesn't play all the positions. A business needs to develop systems and perhaps find additional people that will run the plays for you while you lead.

As a side note, I found that my business never really took off until I found a way to get out of the way. I found as the owner/operator of my business I got caught up in too many details and ran out of time every day. I could not get enough done, and my bottom line suffered. As soon as I found a way to get out of the way and either let a system or a person handle things for me, my business soared. Sometimes when people ask me, "What do you do for a living?" I say, "As little as possible." The truth is my job as a business owner is to lead, and I do that by constantly looking for people to delegate tasks to who can do a far better job than I can.

## Franchising and Licensing

To become a self-made millionaire in business doesn't always require you to come up with a great business idea or start from square one. There are many people who have become self-made millionaires by operating a business system created by someone else. This can be easier for some people, but it can require a significant amount in start-up fees or franchising costs.

There are many differences between franchises and licensing, and many great books have been written on those subjects. For our purposes I simply want to make you aware of those possibilities. If it is something that interests you I would encourage you to seek the advice of your local franchise association, a lawyer and perhaps a mentor who has experience in franchising and licensing.

Before we leave this subject you may also wish to look at your own existing business and explore if it is a good candidate to develop as a franchise that you could offer others. Again it is worth consulting people who are experts in franchise development or licensing to help you explore if that may be a great fit for you.

## From Experience

As far as licensing goes, as I have developed films like *The Opus, The Gratitude Experiment* or even some of our coaching programs, we have offered licensing opportunities to others. For us, licensing has been a great way to capitalize on our intellectual property and grow our brand. When we licensed the book version of *The Opus* I soon found my book in more than twenty-three countries and languages around the world. Immediately it generated an international audience and laid the foundation for future business in each of those territories.

Currently we offer many licensing opportunities for many of our programs. Who knows, maybe we can be business partners in the future through one of our opportunities? Check out our Web site to learn more.

## Technology and Innovation

Technology is a significant part of our world. It is connected to nearly every facet of our lives. It is safe to say then that if you are on the cutting edge of technology there can be some serious money made. The only challenge is that technology is always changing at lightning fast speed.

I recently read an interview with a leading technology expert. The interviewer asked, "What do you think the future will look like?" To that the expert responded, "Thirty-five percent of us are already there. The rest of you will catch up in about two to three years."

Being on the cutting edge of change is a great place to be.

## Caution

Having raised capital for many technology ideas in the past I do have a word of caution. Technology changes so fast that if you want any hope of making money here you have to be fast to market. Generally the product first to market with the newest technology owns that space. Think of the iPod, for example. Apple was first to market, yet many others tried to bring their own version of an MP3 player or some other digital device afterwards. None of them were ever able to compete with Apple.

It can take a lot of money, energy and drive to be first to the marketplace and to own that space. In some cases it doesn't matter if you're first, either. Some of the technology on the market can be duplicated and if high demand exists, that market can become oversaturated.

Most of the technology we have been involved in raising capital for has a really difficult time in the marketplace. In fact, it is so difficult that I rarely commit to technology projects anymore.

For example, several years ago I was approached by a company that had a new system to implement text to smartphone marketing. They wanted me to raise them some money.

The idea was simple—they had the ability to send text messages to databases. They could send everything from coupons to daily success quotes. These text messages to the general public would be available by paid subscription only. On the surface it looked like there could be thousands of potential users and millions of dollars in potential revenue. Who wouldn't want coupons sent to their phone, right? This company was very optimistic and felt that they could be ready to go to market in six months to a year.

**What would You do?**

I decided to pass. I am glad I did. They were not quite the first to market, and in a very short time the entire arena of text-based marketing became oversaturated. Instead of being excited to get coupons on their phone, people started to feel like they were getting flyers in their mailbox. Don't we call that junk mail, or on the Internet, spam? Who would pay for that? At last count I found on Google more than 5 thousand companies offering text-based marketing. In order to make a significant amount of money in technology, you can't afford to have that much competition.

**Innovation**

Innovation essentially means to find something that already exists and make it better. I would like emphasize that it's even smarter to not just take something, but take something that works and make it work better.

Many of today's most successful businesses are innovations on ideas that were already in the marketplace. Innovators improved on ideas that had already proved viable. Consider the following innovations:

- FedEx—an innovation on UPS or the US postal service
- Facebook—an innovation on MySpace and several other social networking sites

- Walmart—an innovation on department stores
- Apple—an innovation on a variety of other computer brands

I could go on and on.

The principle of innovation isn't new, however. Innovating is as old as time and has been the resource for many of the important things we take for granted every day in our lives. Let me point out one example by introducing you to the king of all innovators, as far as I'm concerned. His name was Thomas Edison.

Most people consider him the greatest inventor of all time, but that just isn't true. Here are some of the things that he is credited for bringing to market. Notice the original patent dates and who first registered them. Then look at the date that Thomas Edison brought them to the world.

### Electric Lightbulb

Sir Joseph Wilson Swan first demonstrated his new invention, the lightbulb, on December 18, 1878, in England. Edison's first US patent on the lightbulb was, in fact, a direct copy of Swan's first prototype. Edison and Swan partnered to sell the lightbulb in 1883, creating The Ediswan Light Co. In 1892 this company became Edison General Electric.

### Phonograph

While the phonograph produced by Edison was a significant innovation on existing sound-recording devices, they were mere innovations on recorders produced by Édouard-Léon Scott de Martinville and Charles Cros. Edison built on their ideas and was first to market with a more advanced version of a sound-recording machine, which he called a phonograph, in 1877.

## Motion Picture Camera

The first patent filed on a motion-picture camera was for a design by Louis Le Prince in 1888 in England. Several years later, in 1891, Edison filed a patent in the United States for his version of the camera and called it a kinetographic camera. Although many people feel that Edison invented motion pictures, there were many patents filed after his patent with vast improvements on his original design. Today most motion picture equipment is more similar to the other patents than to Edison's efforts in motion picture technology. Yet he is still credited by many as being the inventor.

Caution: Just because you have an idea to innovate something doesn't mean you should. Innovation is not a guarantee of success. Thomas Edison filed over 1093 patents during his lifetime. There are many items that he tried to develop over the years. For one example, he was very interested in developing a new process for mining iron ore. After a short period of interest he decided for one reason or another that either the timing wasn't right or that the market wasn't ready.

We'll talk a little later about some questions you might want to answer before bringing an innovation or idea to market.

## A Few Interesting Thoughts on Innovation

Innovation is all about ideas. If you are on the trail to developing something new and exciting in the field of innovation, it is certainly worth consulting a lawyer about your new idea to see how it can be protected as intellectual property.

Once the idea is protected, if it can be, you may not need to develop it. If the idea has merit there can be a lot of money in licensing it to another company to develop. I have licensed intellectual property, and it is not uncommon to receive a licensing fee upfront and then regular royalty payments as the new idea is implemented and becomes profitable. Royalty payments can continue for years and years into the future, and depending on the significance of your innovation, can be very lucrative.

## Infomercials

Infomercials are a brilliant place to sell innovations. Yet you don't have to go on TV to do this. With the Internet, there are now countless ways to share your innovations in a similar format to the one infomercials have been using for years. There is a reason this formula works, and the key is to be creative and find big audiences to share your innovation with.

## Innovation doesn't Just Mean Products

Innovation can occur on just about anything. For example, a business partner and I once hosted a series of quite successful events called "The Art & Entertainment Expo" in my hometown of Calgary, Alberta. The event featured exhibits on comic books, film and TV.

About three or four years after our company changed gears and stopped doing the event, one of our original attendees actually innovated on our original idea and expanded our event to a grander scale. He even kept our original name. I am excited he saw the value in what we did and had the skills to do more with the idea than we did, because it's a great event that thousands of people attend every year. Innovation can be very lucrative.

## One Caution on Innovations

Sometimes an innovative idea may be successful but it's just too new of an idea to catch on. Be sure that if your idea requires specific instructions, training or understanding that you have that built into your marketing plan. Nothing can kill a brilliant idea faster than it being too complex to implement.

## Innovation doesn't mean you have to come up with the best ideas yourself

One of the great things about innovation is that if you listen carefully to people around you, you can find out what people really want. In fact, your greatest seeds for success can be gained by listening to what other people want.

Great innovations also come from bringing something you might have seen elsewhere in the world to your own backyard. There are many great opportunities that saw their beginnings in Europe, Asia or Australia and that are now great successes in the United States and vice versa.

## Investments

According to the United States Census Bureau, approximately 16% of self-made millionaires are created through the investment category.[2] Most of these investors arrive at their million through a combination of several activities. Most often these activities involve investing directly in business and entrepreneurship. Often, they arrive at millionaire status through real estate investments.

While most investments look really good on paper, one common danger is that they do not always provide a regular cash flow. I encourage students to look for cash flow investments where possible. As mentioned earlier in the book, cash flow will be the only factor that changes your life experience. But cash flow is also a way to keep better tabs on the company you've invested in. If it has trouble paying regular dividends, this can often be a sign that the company is in trouble.

To invest *means to place funds in a state of potential growth.*

## Myth 1

Saving is not investing. Too often people confuse saving with investing. To save is to hold money or put it aside. To invest means to place funds in a state of potential growth.

**Myth 2**

Generally, to participate in the investment category, most people think that they have to have a ton of money to begin. This is not true. There are various investment opportunities, like real estate for example, where you can utilize money from other people, banks or other sources. If you are considering stock trading there are options available to you that allow you to trade stocks valued at just a penny.

**Myth 3**

It is hard to find good investments. First, let's talk about what a good investment is. To me, a good investment is one that is secure, has a reasonable, if not great, return potential and does not take too much time to yield returns.

If an investment has the following three things, I consider it worth exploring.

**Manageable Risk**

You'll remember earlier we talked about the word *risk*. I felt that the word *evaluation* was better suited to describing investments. The reason is that the more experience you gain, the more you are able to evaluate and manage risk.

**Exceptional Return**

There are many places to put your money, and all of them have different potential rates of return. Generally, but not always, the return is based on a few things.

1. The level of risk involved
2. The time frame of the investment
3. How desperately the opportunity needs to be funded

There is no such thing as a fixed rate in a private offering. Those creating the offering try to build the rates of return to be as attractive as possible to potential investors and still leave room to make money themselves with the venture. In private offerings, it is important to remember that these rates can sometimes be negotiable. When you are the one with the money, oftentimes the negotiating power is entirely in your hands.

## Reasonable Time

I try to find investments that will provide a return to me in a reasonable time. I do not like having my money tied up for long periods of time. Very rarely, for example, will I participate in land development deals which can often take up to ten or more years to develop. I prefer quicker opportunities where I can expect my money back inside of three to five years or less.

The myth that there are few great investments that fit these categories is baloney. There are many investment opportunities everywhere that meet these criteria. Read Myth 3 again—it is hard to find good investments. The problem isn't that there aren't any good investments. The problem may be finding them. Unless you know where to look and what you are looking for, you may not recognize them.

Plato's Socrates said, "If you live in a cave all you see is shadows." Meaning that what you surround yourself with dictates what you will see around you. If you are not seeing the investment opportunities you want to see, you need to change your surroundings. Once you change your surroundings, new opportunities will appear.

## Additional Ways People have Become Millionaires

Before I share these ways people have become self-made millionaires, let's just be clear that these are not recommendations. But they are kind of interesting.

- Married a millionaire (It happens every day.)
- Inherited the money
- Won the lottery
- Won it gambling (It is said that more than $30 million changes hands in Las Vegas casinos every hour.)
- Won a game show
- Discovered valuable collectibles at garage sales (Google this and you'll be surprised at how often it happens.)
- Helped Donald Trump with roadside assistance (In a January 2005 episode of *The Apprentice*, Donald Trump said that someone helped him with roadside assistance, and in return he paid off their mortgage.)

And lastly,

- Got their picture taken with an alien and sold it to the *National Enquirer* (This actually happened by the way. The *National Enquirer* paid $1 million for a photo of an alleged alien that came to a man's doorstep, claiming to be from the planet Zifron.)

## EXERCISES

1. Is there a business idea you have had for a long time that you would like to develop? Consider what the potential for real profitability and growth is. If the idea has limits, you may want to reconsider. Also remember that a business idea that requires you to be there for every minute of every day is not in a strong position to create the greatest wealth. More on this in future chapters.

2. Does your business have intellectual property that can be licensed? If so, what aspects could be licensed? What is the procedure and what are the costs? What support would you be able to provide?

3. Think about a highly successful idea in the marketplace right now. Is there a way that you could innovate the idea to make it more effective, exciting, profitable, easier to use or more cost effective?

4. Listen to the concerns and complaints of others. Take careful mental notes. What solutions can you think of for some of these issues? How can you solve these problems at a profit?

5. Make a commitment to invest a portion of your funds in your financial future. In a future chapter I will share with you how much you might want to consider investing. But for now, make the commitment. I did not say *"save."* Saving and investing are very different. To save means to put away or preserve. It doesn't mean to hold or place funds in a state of growth. To invest is to place funds in a state of potential growth.

6. This is an exercise I use in the seminars I teach. Fill in the blank: I made my fortune by_____
_____. Be as specific as you can. When you know the answer to the blank, begin to spend time becoming an expert in that area. For example, if you chose real estate, start learning everything you can about real estate. If you chose a specific kind of business, do everything you can to learn all the aspects of that business. What you learn will have a direct effect on what you are able to earn.

## QUESTIONS

Consider the questions below that fit best with the area you are most interested in.

### Business and Entrepreneurship

1. What business are you engaged in currently?
2. What problems do you solve?

3. What are the major problems you could service that you are not currently addressing?
4. What possibilities are there for recurring revenue streams?
5. Are you getting an effective return on your efforts?
6. Are you running or leading your business?
7. Who could be a helpful part of your team?
8. How could you make your business more profitable?
9. Do you have a plan for growth? What is it?
10. Can your business be franchised or licensed?
11. Who can help you set up your franchise or license?

## Technology and Innovation

1. What around you needs to be innovated or made easier?
2. How fast can you get to market?
3. Where are the markets that need your innovation?
4. Can they easily understand how to use your innovation?
5. How can you target them?
6. What problems are crying out for a solution that you could get to work on?
7. What activities in your community could be innovated for the better?

## Investment

1. When looking at a possible investment opportunity consider the following:
   - What is the potential return?
   - How long will it take?
   - What is the potential risk?
   - Where in your city might you go to discover new or better investment opportunities?

# PART 2

## Money and How You can Join the Millionaires Club

# What You Believe about Money Matters

WHERE DO MOST PEOPLE get their ideas about money? Where did you get your ideas about money? If you are like most people, your ideas about money came from your parents. Often, the ideas that most parents leave their children are not much more than the advice to balance your check book, live within a budget and stay out of debt. That advice isn't going to make you rich.

The reason most parents aren't giving better advice is that they just don't know what to share. Let's be honest. If you look at the financial situation that most parents are in, they aren't creating extraordinary abundance. They are most likely running their lives in the way most of the rest of America is. The average annual income for most American households is $51,548 per year. The average American has $1,311 in a savings account. And most don't have any more than $2,500 invested in some form of retirement savings plan. The majority of people in the United States are very ill-equipped to be giving financial advice to anyone.

Before we blame our parents for the advice they have given us, let's think for a minute about where they got the wisdom they are sharing. Any ideas? You got it. From their parents.

And if you trace that advice back it will go on for generations. Not only did your parents not know how to become rich themselves, but they did know what to tell you. Even if they did know what created wealth in the 1980s or 1990s, those rules don't apply anymore.

Coincidentally, I recently spoke at a conference at a business school. One of the discussion points was the speed of change. I want to share a few points from the discussion to emphasize how important it is that we always try to develop, especially in the area of finance and wealth growth.

To begin the discussion of change, we talked about how music is listened to. We asked the oldest man, one of the teachers in the room, about how he listened to music while he was in high school. He shared that it was a record called either a 78 rpm, a 33rpm or a 45rpm. Most of the college-age students had no idea what he was talking about. We then talked about the next evolution in music listening.

Another professor raised her hand and mentioned eight-track tapes; another professor then talked about cassette tapes. It was interesting to watch the confused looks on the faces of the students. Another professor then discussed the invention of the compact disc, and finally I started to see a lightbulb of recognition ignite in the eyes of the students. Next, the students started talking about how music is now downloaded over the Internet and stored on phones and iPods.

The reason I mention this evolution is to demonstrate that change happens. And in the field of wealth growth there have been incredible changes in the ways money is made and managed. Back to my original question—where did you learn about money? Your parents. And where did they learn about money? Their parents and so on and so on back to the biblical times. Do you think anything has changed since then? Absolutely.

The big problem for many people when it comes to growing wealth is that they are operating with outdated ideas on what money is, how it is made and how to grow financial abundance. In Chapter Six we will focus more on the kind of thinking that is required to become a self-made millionaire, but for now let's talk about the power of belief on your ability to be financially abundant.

## WHAT YOU BELIEVE ABOUT MONEY MAKES A DIFFERENCE

Generally speaking, everything we do is motivated by our beliefs in a future outcome. Many of these beliefs come from our past experience, but many of them come from expectations we may have formed from our interactions with others. What others say, especially when the information comes from people we trust or respect, has a significant impact on what we believe. But is this information always correct? Of course not.

In fact, many of the things that we believe and accept as true are quite often proven false later on down the road. (Remember when most people thought the earth was flat?)

Believing a false idea, like that the world is flat, can limit our ability to be successful and to progress. I'd like to share several false beliefs that people have about money. (If you'd like to learn more about these beliefs and how to overcome them (if you have them), check out my book *The Millionaire Myth: 21 Beliefs About Money that Keep You from Being Rich*.) You might want to put a check mark next to the beliefs you currently have about money.

- ❑ There's not enough to go around.
- ❑ I don't have access to opportunities to make money.
- ❑ Not everyone can be rich.
- ❑ Money doesn't bring happiness.
- ❑ Money is the root of all evil. (Rich people are crooks.)
- ❑ Money corrupts people.
- ❑ Rich people only care about themselves or their money.
- ❑ Other people will think badly of me if I get too rich.
- ❑ Rich people aren't spiritual.
- ❑ I shouldn't get my hopes up—most times things fail.
- ❑ Be realistic.
- ❑ I'm not a Rockefeller.
- ❑ Money doesn't grow on trees.
- ❑ I need to have money to make money.

- ☐ It may work for others, but it won't work for me. (I'm not lucky.)
- ☐ Who do I think I am? I'm not really rich. I shouldn't act like I am.
- ☐ I will have to sacrifice too much to get there.
- ☐ I should be content with what I have. (And not envy or covet what I don't have.)
- ☐ The richest people are born into money.
- ☐ I will have to take big risks to get big returns
- ☐ If I get rich I won't be able to manage the money.
- ☐ If I make more money I will have to pay it back in taxes.
- ☐ There is a limit to how much money I am entitled to.
- ☐ I need money to solve money problems.

Each of these common beliefs is limiting and will keep you from creating a life of abundance. Wealth and abundance are something that everyone deserves to have. They are not reserved for only a specific few; they are available to all who wish to have them as part of their lives.

Let's take a minute and review a few of these beliefs quickly and discuss some of the errors in this kind of thinking. Again, for a more comprehensive discussion on these beliefs and how to overcome them, please read my book *The Millionaire Myth: 21 Beliefs About Money that Keep You from Being Rich*. Here are four of the most common false beliefs about money that I regularly encounter.

### There's not Enough to Go Around

The idea of scarcity has been around a long time. The phrase *scarcity mentality* is fairly recent. It is a phrase first used by Thomas Malthus, a British economist who lived in India in the late 1700s. While he was there he noted that the population of India was growing so quickly there was a definite danger that there could be a shortage of food in the near future. Many subscribed to his theories. The only thing that he and his followers did not take into consideration was mankind's ability to solve problems. Since Malthus's day, mankind has discovered many methods to increase food production, preserve existing food supplies and transport food to different parts of the globe.

While this theory of scarcity has existed in the minds of men since the dawn of time, very rarely has there ever been a situation where scarcity has existed long term.

Generally speaking, the planet has always found a way to provide when individuals learn the principles of how to tap into its available abundance. Scarcity never has a permanent grip on our lives except as we allow it to.

## Not Everyone can be Rich

Not everyone can be rich. While this may be true, I would suggest that the other side of this coin must also be true: not everyone can be poor. If poverty and abundance must, out of necessity, exist, doesn't it sound fair to suggest that whichever side of the coin you are on will be determined by how well you apply the principles that create that particular circumstance.

Something that most people forget is that becoming and staying poor also requires effort. And surprisingly, the amount of effort needed to be rich is almost the same. The real difference between the rich and the poor is found in how they structure and systematize their lives. Other than that, both groups have the same number of hours in a day, both have ups and downs and both put their pants on one leg at a time. Ultimately, you need to make a choice. And that choice really comes down to how you choose to spend your time. You get to choose which side of the coin you will be on.

## You Need to Have Money to Make Money

This is the number-one thing I hear regularly that keeps people from changing their financial situation. Specifically, when it comes to investing or purchasing assets that will grow wealth, people commonly say that they are waiting until they have a little more money to get started. The truth of the matter is that every little penny makes a difference. Here's a little exercise to remind you of the value of a penny. In our seminars we often ask the question: which would you rather have—a check for $3 million or the results of your money doubling every day for thirty days, starting with a penny? Most people say, "Duh … The $3 million, of course." Then we ask them to look at the following table.

Figure 5.1: Money doubled every day starting with a penny

| Day | |
|---|---|
| 1 | .01¢ |
| 2 | .02¢ |
| 3 | .04¢ |
| 4 | .08¢ |
| 5 | .16¢ |
| 6 | .32¢ |
| 7 | .64¢ |
| 8 | $1.28 |
| 9 | $2.56 |
| 10 | $5.12 |
| 11 | $10.24 |
| 12 | $20.48 |
| 13 | $40.96 |
| 14 | $81.20 |
| 15 | $163.84 |
| 16 | $327.68 |
| 17 | $655.36 |
| 18 | $1,310.72 |
| 19 | $2,621.44 |
| 20 | $5,242.88 |

| Day | |
|-----|-------------|
| 21 | $10,485.76 |
| 22 | $20,971.52 |
| 23 | $41,943.04 |
| 24 | $83,886.08 |
| 25 | $167,772.16 |
| 26 | $335,544.32 |
| 27 | $671,088.64 |
| 28 | $1,342,177.28 |
| 29 | $2,684,354.56 |
| 30 | $5,368,709.12 |

We often neglect the small things because we think we need big things to make a difference. *The truth is that we can't get to the big things until we take care of the little things.* If you don't value a small amount of money, you will never get the opportunity to manage a big amount of money. A small amount of money correctly utilized over time can make an incredible difference.

You've probably heard the idea that the final destination of a ship can be changed entirely by simply shifting its heading by a degree. The same holds true for your financial future. If you start with the small things and remain consistent, the end result will be incredible.

*Most people are robbed of large fortunes
because they neglect little things.*

I want to share another idea about the false impression that you need money to make money. Money is most often generated where there is a need to be filled or a problem to be solved. In other words, the abundance in your life right now is a reflection of your ability to be of service to others.

When I first started in business I discovered a set of needs I could easily service. My greatest strength is working with people. I am good at meeting them, interacting with them and helping them find others who can help solve their problems. I noticed that there are many people looking for money in the world. They are looking for money to buy a house, start a business, pay some bills, buy a car. They need money for whatever it is that they are trying to do.

I also found that there are many people with money who are looking to invest or lend money if the right opportunity comes along.

When I recognized this I saw an opportunity. It could be highly profitable for me to find a way to introduce these two kinds of people to each other. I designed a strategy whereby I could introduce the people who needed the money to those who had the money, and I would get paid by both of them. In fact, I got paid 20% by each of them, which meant I made 40% on the entire deal. You can run the numbers. If the project involved $100 thousand, I would make $40 thousand. I might add that many of these deals, especially when people needed the money for business or real estate, far exceeded $100 thousand. It was a great way for me to make some extra money and it didn't cost me anything.

Money can be made without money. The key factor in creating wealth is that it requires resourcefulness more than resources.

### Money can't Solve Money Problems

Why can't money solve money problems? Because it's rare that money problems are created by money.

Money problems are created by how one thinks about and uses their resources. Most people don't think carefully about their future. They don't plan or prepare for it, and so when it arrives they find themselves in trouble. As a future millionaire you need to think carefully about the future and learn to anticipate what is coming. When you learn to think and prepare better for the future, you will find that your money problems will begin to disappear.

The majority of money problems come from a lack of planning, not from a lack of money.

Think about it. It's not necessarily how much you make that takes away your money problems. There are people, celebrities are often a good example, who make incredible amounts of money yet still have very serious money problems. It isn't how much you make, but how you think, plan, prepare and ultimately spend your money that makes the biggest difference in how much you will have at the end of the day.

In order to create solutions to the financial challenges you may currently face, you will have to look at those situations from a different point of view than you used to create them.

*No problem can be solved from the same level of consciousness that created it.*
—Albert Einstein

I would add to Einstein's thought that in order to fix the problem, and I am talking permanently, you will also need to change your actions. We will talk a little more about millionaire habits in the next chapter.

## GOOD SOURCES TO CONSULT ABOUT MONEY

### Financial Education Programs

There are great financial education opportunities available almost everywhere. But that doesn't mean they are all of equal value. Be careful about who is delivering this financial education to you. Just because someone has studied financial strategy in a classroom does not mean they are qualified to guide others in real life. I recently read a report about financial planners in Canada and the United States. The report indicated that 80% of them have less money than the people they are giving advice to. Most of them have never earned over $100 thousand a year. If your goal is to be a millionaire, you need to take advice from someone who is already there.

Most of the financial planners in the business today direct people to purchase products that pay themselves a high commission but don't necessarily have customers' best interests in mind. Most financial planners also don't have real estate, buying and selling business, exempt market or private equity type products available for you to invest in. In most cases, these are the kinds of deals that you will need to become rich.

Diversification is one of the key features that has made my program, Millionaire Training Systems, so successful. My team and I diversify the kinds of offerings we help people find, and most importantly, ALL of the mentors helping our students are actually earning over $1 million annually. And the licensed coaches that are sharing our one-on-one tools are trained directly by myself or one of our millionaire mentors and have their direct support to help you grow. Our strategies work in the real world and are not just theory.

*What you learn is directly tied to what you will earn*

### Other Millionaires and High Net Worth Individuals

If you wanted to be a gifted painter, you wouldn't study painting with a carpenter, would you? It only makes sense then that if you would be a millionaire you need to start spending time with, and learning from, millionaires and other high net worth individuals.

Even if the millionaires you are spending time with do not sit down with you in a formal classroom setting, you can still learn tons by just associating with them. Again, you'll remember we talked about the principle of probability. The more time you spend with millionaires, doing the kinds of things they do, the greater your chances are of aligning your life to get the results that they are getting.

As I learned this principle of association in my early twenties, I found that I immediately began to think differently about money, and also began to hear of opportunities that really made a difference to my bottom line.

By the way, it is very interesting to me to observe what different people view as a high net worth individual. I have seen many who haven't been surrounded by wealth in the past label people who make

$100 thousand annually as high net worth individuals. I wouldn't agree and I would caution you not to put just anyone up on the high net worth pedestal. Be sure they've earned the right to be there. If you aim low and aspire low, you will remain low. If you shoot high, you will reach high. Aim so high that it seems near impossible you will achieve anything, and you will really make a difference in your end result. I like the saying: "Aim for the moon and you'll end up living among the stars." Aim high, and even if you only get partway there, you will still have an incredible experience. Aim low and you will achieve it, but you will become only a portion of what you are destined to become.

**Mentors**

Mentors are a significant source of wealth learning. A good mentor, however, is very difficult to find. A mentor is very different from a coach. I like the example a friend of mine, Joseph McClendon III, once shared with me. "The basketball player Michael Jordan had a coach. But that coach," he said, "was not a better basketball player than Michael Jordan. The coach was valuable but had limitations. Michael Jordan, on the other hand, could be a good mentor, specifically because he had been the best and knew all the experiences of what it took to be the best."

The same is true of wealth building. Mentors are better than coaches. Mentors come from a place of experience, not of theory.

You want to entrust your financial future to people who have experience and wisdom that can make a difference for you. Your money is valuable and should not be entrusted to just anyone. If you want to have a significant improvement in your financial situation, you should be on the lookout for the best people to help you, and make special efforts to learn from them.

**Does Financial Education Cost or Pay?**

Too often people forget that every purchase they make is an investment. Everything you buy gives a return, as we mentioned at the beginning of this book. It will either increase your quality of life, enable you to create or allow you to contribute. The investment in your financial education will also give you the ability to progress in these three areas.

If you want to be financially free, you must learn what it will take for you to arrive at that destination.

Many people look at the price of financial education both in dollars and time and become frightened that the burden is too big. I would strongly state that the price of ignorance is where the real cost is. Ignorance limits your ability to see things as they really are and to utilize tools that you may not yet be aware of. Often we forget how lessons early in our lives changed our lives. If you had never learned how to walk, tie your shoes or ride a bike, your freedom and opportunities would be extremely limited. The same is true of financial education. The more you learn the more power and ability you have.

*The more you learn the more you earn.*

Before each of our seminars we have participants complete a quick questionnaire. Question 6 reads as follows:

If you could learn how to make an extra $25,000-$75,000 or more per year for the rest of your life, what would that be worth to you?
$10,000 ☐    $25,000 ☐    $35,000 ☐    $50,000 ☐    $100,000 ☐

Go ahead. Check the box with the dollar amount you would be willing to pay for that information before reading further. This will reveal a little bit about you and how serious you are about building your wealth.

Let's just say you had another twenty years to live and let's be modest, let's say I taught you how to make only $25 thousand extra a year, how much would that be? That's $500 thousand!

Would you believe that I have people who check they would be willing to pay only $10 thousand for that information? Even at $100 thousand, that investment would pay incredible dividends.

What did you choose? If you are really committed to becoming wealthy, you see a even $100 thousand price tag as an irresistible opportunity. I think the problem comes down to this. Let me illustrate with a story from my own experience. When I was first starting out as an investor in my early twenties, before investing, I would always ask, "How much does it cost?" or "What's the minimum investment?"

One day one of my mentors heard me ask this question and scolded me. He did it kindly, but it was a scolding. He said, "You are asking the wrong question. Who cares what it costs?" I must have looked at him with a surprised look on my face because he began to illustrate. "If something costs $10 thousand and you lose it all, does it matter what it cost?" I shook my head. Of course it didn't. I had lost $10 thousand. He continued. "If something costs $1 million and you make $3 million, does it matter what it costs?" I shook my head again. With that opportunity I would have made $2 million. He smiled as he saw I was getting the lesson. "The better question, then, isn't how much does it cost, but how much do I stand to make?"

Financial education isn't about how much it costs. It's about how much you stand to make. If I could teach you how to make an extra $25 thousand to $75 thousand every single year for the rest of your life, does it really matter how much it costs?

Financial education is priceless. It allows you to become more resourceful and recognize opportunities. Resourcefulness and recognizing possibilities are the keys to making big deals happen. When you know how to play by the rules then you can start getting creative and working on the stuff that goes beyond the basics. That is where the real money is.

All top athletes learn the basics before they learn the extraordinary stuff that makes them superstars. The same is true with wealth building. Learn as much as you can about the basics, and suddenly you will begin to develop the ideas and skills that will grow your wealth in extraordinary ways.

## EXERCISES

1.  Evaluate your thoughts and beliefs about money and eliminate any that are not serving you.

2. Remember always that the seemingly small stuff matters. Where is your money disappearing on small things you don't think matter? How can you make adjustments to start using your money better? Make a plan to take care of the small stuff and stick to it.
3. Seek out ways to increase your financial education. Where can you go to start increasing your financial education immediately?
4. Where can you go to start spending more time with high net worth individuals today? If you want some help with ideas for this, a valuable resource is my book *Network like a Millionaire*. It shares some of the most important strategies and techniques for creating relationships with rich, famous and vital people to help you grow your net worth.
5. Lastly, it is important that you find a mentor and follow their advice.

## Additional Considerations

Consider what you currently believe about money and think carefully about where that belief came from. Are these beliefs serving you?

Resourcefulness is what grows wealth. What creative ideas can you come up with right now? The more powerful and interesting your ideas, the more people will pay to participate.

What money problems are you currently experiencing? How could these problems be fixed or prevented through thinking, planning and preparing differently? How could you alter your spending to provide better solutions for your money issues?

## QUESTIONS

1. Money doubled every day for thirty days, starting with 1¢ or $3 million. What would you choose?
2. Why and how does this lesson fit into day-to-day wealth building?

3. What small adjustments can you make in your financial life to be better right now?
4. What are you currently doing to learn more about correct ideas regarding money?
5. Where could you learn more about correct ideas regarding money?
6. What negative things do you believe about money?
7. Why do you believe these things? What power is this belief taking away from you?
8. What positive things do you believe about money?
9. How are these beliefs giving you financial power?
10. How can you strengthen these beliefs?
11. How can you be resourceful with your current situation to make it more profitable?
12. What can you change in your thinking, planning, preparation and actions that will start to give you better results in your financial life?
13. What is your idea of a high net worth individual?
14. How high are you aiming currently? (Remember, be specific and clear.)
15. Where will you find an appropriate mentor?

# The Keys to Millionaire Thinking

YOUR THINKING IS SO IMPORTANT to creating wealth. It cannot be stressed enough. If you think or believe that you can't be successful in wealth creation, you won't even get to the starting line.

When I was a young college student I remember pleading with a friend of mine for some advice to get me out of all the debt I was accumulating through student loans. His response was, "It's all in your head." At the time I thought he was being rude and didn't understand my situation. But since then I have come to understand that he was exactly right. If you can't get your head figured out correctly, meaning your thinking, you have no hope of changing your financial situation.

*You can only find what you are looking for.*

Millionaire thinking is important. Remember the Albert Einstein quote from Chapter 5, that "a problem cannot be solved at the same level of thinking that created it." Einstein recognized there are different levels of thinking. The reason most people have money problems is that they look at money problems with the same level of thinking that was used to create them. In order to get out of money problems you need to look at money problems from a higher level. I call that level of thinking abundance thinking or millionaire thinking.

Millionaire thinking recognizes solutions and is hopeful even in a challenging circumstance. Millionaire thinking is proactive, not reactive. Millionaire thinking looks to the future rather than griping about the past. Millionaire thinking tries to think of a positive thing to do with spilled milk rather than cry over the fact that it's been spilled. We will talk more about what this mind-set is and how to develop it through the course of this chapter.

I encourage you to make a commitment this instant to do whatever you can to put yourself into the millionaire mind-set. Solution and positive hope are the new order of the day.

## Competing Thoughts

It is estimated that each day we have more than 70 thousand unique thoughts. If you do the math, that comes down to about 2,916 per hour and 48.6 per minute. That's a lot of thinking. Especially when you consider that our thoughts are extremely important to our success.

Our thoughts dictate our actions and behaviors, which in turn generate our results. If you want to change the quality of your results, you must first start by improving the quality of your thoughts.

The same study that gave us the information about how many thoughts we have each day also confirms that the majority of the thoughts we have each day are not empowering us. In fact, it is estimated that more than 70% of the thoughts the average person has each day are negative, reactionary or just plain neutral. These are the kinds of thoughts that keep most people from creating greater abundance in their lives.

Millionaires think differently. It's as simple as that. They are not just positive thinkers, although that is important. They are actually empowered or proactive thinkers.

They plan ahead, think ahead and pursue with determination the things that they want. This determined kind of thinking is more than just a belief that they can succeed. They actually decide ahead of time that the outcome they will achieve is success, and all their thought energy goes toward creating that outcome in the real world.

A lot of people claim that they believe they can be successful, but that's not enough. They need to create actions to demonstrate those beliefs are real. Actions are the manifestation of true beliefs. What you think about most and then act on becomes your reality.

Financial success will only come if you make it a priority among your thoughts and actions.

Before we talk about actions, let's talk about a few keys to creating stronger and more frequent thoughts about greater abundance in your life. Here are three significant keys.

## Key One: Clarity

Often we hear that success clarity is a matter of determining our destination with clarity. I think that this is important, but I also believe it is incomplete. In addition to knowing where you want to go, you also need to know the first step to take.

The old Chinese proverb that states the journey of a thousand miles begins with a single footstep could well be rewritten: "The journey to where you want to go begins with a single footstep in the right direction." When we have clarity on where we are going and the first steps we take are in the right direction, we may very well find that the journey isn't a thousand miles after all.

*A goal that is specific and clear becomes attainable and near*

The challenge that most people experience is that they do not have clear financial goals. They plan only as far as their next paycheck and even then, when it arrives, it is often spent well before they can kick their plan into gear.

*No plan = financial chaos*

In order to get clear about what you want to do with your money, you need a plan that applies to right now. A plan that is far in the distance and doesn't translate to today can lack power. Your plan should help you see the future, but you should be able to break it down into measurable things you can do each day.

When I began working on my first million I even broke my plan down into what I needed to accomplish financially each day, each hour and yes, it may sound a bit too detailed, but even each moment. It worked out to $2,739 a day, $114 an hour (24 hours a day) and $1.90 per minute.

Naturally, most of my money did not come to me by the minute, hour or even day, but having the breakdown of these goals kept me on track. This clarity gave me a constant reminder that helped control my spending and my use of time, and helped me to always keep my eye on the bigger picture.

If those numbers sound ambitious for you, start with a number that is more realistic for you but not too easy. In order to become rich you need a goal that will stretch you beyond your current income level. On the other hand, don't bite off more than you can chew. It is not a race to get to a million. Consistency in effort and focus is the key. Perhaps start with a smaller amount to create $10 thousand or $20 thousand a month, and then build it up from there.

### Key Two: Emotional Commitment, Social Congruency and Your Logical Brain

We often hear about how brain science and new discoveries about the brain affect all the aspects of our lives. It seems that the more we understand about the brain, the more power we have to use our thoughts to our advantage.

As we become more aware of how our brain works and sorts information, we discover the real reasons why we sometimes fail to reach our most important goals, and what we can do about it. It's time to get scientific for a moment.

According to neuroscientists, our brain can be divided into three major areas when it comes to sorting information. These areas are known as the reptilian brain or emotive brain, the mammalian or social brain and the cognitive or logical brain. Here's a brief, simple description about each of these areas.

Reptilian or emotive brain. This part of the brain controls our emotional drives.

Mammalian or social brain. This part of our brain allows us to work in groups or cooperate socially.

Cognitive or logical brain. This is the part of our brain that makes logical decisions.

Each of these brain areas builds upon, and is subject to, the one before it. Think of it like floors in a house. The foundation is the emotive brain, the main floor is the social brain and the upstairs is the logical brain. If you took away the foundation of the house, all the floors above it would fall. If you took away the main floor, the upstairs would come crashing down.

The same is true when attempting to achieve financial goals or whatever else we may be attempting to achieve. Let's use some real life examples to illustrate.

**Example 1: Emotional Brain versus Logical Brain**

Let's say logically you set the goal to save $200 a month from your current pay check and redirect this money to investments. This happens in your logical brain. Saving $200 is a logical idea that you know will give you benefit. But all of a sudden, your emotional brain is activated by a purchase choice that comes along that sure is tempting. On a visit to the mall you find an incredible treasure—a pair of irresistible brand-name jeans, and the best news is that they are on sale. Normally $300 jeans and they are on for $199. After some struggle between the jeans and your investment decision (but not much struggle), you try on the jeans. Naturally, they fit perfectly, and soon they are in your closet at home. Round one goes to your emotional brain.

This happens all the time. Our emotional decisions move us

from what we know we logically need or want to do. We will share some strategies to try to beat this in a minute.

### Example 2: Logical Brain versus Social Brain

Let's try this again to demonstrate our point. Here's the scenario: You know you have a huge bonus coming. You are expecting that it will be around $2,500. You have been researching for a while and have found an investment opportunity that will pay you 12% annually. You don't really need the bonus money anywhere else, and so you have decided with your logical brain that this investment is a perfect contribution to your future wealthier self. But days before you get your bonus a group of your friends decides to go to Vegas on a whim. Naturally, they want you along and start sharing their thoughts on how much fun it will be. And as you weigh the opportunity and recognize that your bonus would cover the entire trip, the group begins to chant, "Vegas! Vegas! Vegas!" Do you think you would go? Of course you would.

Round two to the social brain. The logical brain didn't have a chance. How often do we see peer pressure take over what we logically know we should do or need to do?

In my own life I can think of many experiences where such battles have been fought and lost. As I am writing this, I had one such memory come to mind. This one is particularly sensitive for me because I did something that really challenged me financially.

When I was sixteen, I had a job at a hardware store. I made about $350 a month. I was saving for a car and had $1000 saved. Finally I found a used car that would suit me perfectly, and the price tag was just right at $1250. I could buy it with my next pay check, and that was just days away. My logical brain was ready to make a purchase. Then the most subtle of combined emotional and social attacks took place. And as usually happens to most teenage boys, this story involves a girl. As soon as she came into the picture, the entire plan became disrupted.

This was a girl I really wanted to impress. And wouldn't you know, I met her just before her birthday. To make matters worse, I heard from a friend that she had been asking about me. Well, that was it. I decided to ask her out, and the next thing you know I was also going to her birthday party. Naturally, I wanted to make a good impression, so there it was: my first $600 birthday present. I bought her a small diamond necklace and a leather jacket. And with that present my logical ideas for the car were shattered.

The thing that is interesting to me still is she never asked for or expected such a present. But my feelings of wanting to be significant at her party (social pressure) and my desire to be liked by her (emotional brain) made me forget all of my logical ideas.

### Example 3: Emotional and Social Brain Wins Again

I kind of like my brother's philosophy about dating. He was a bit of a Scrooge in his teenage years, and when I asked him once why he didn't spend money on his dates, he said, "I am not going to marry this one. Why do I want to spend all my money on somebody else's wife?" Kinda makes sense to me.

And that philosophy provides a little bit of a key to overcoming the tendency to fall into the emotional or social brain challenges. That solution is to think the situation through. What will the end result be? If you can find the ability to think situations through, your logical brain may get a fighting chance.

As I conduct my seminars, I notice that one of the biggest challenges that most people have in getting their logical brain to take control deals with the challenge of impulse shopping. It is a common problem around the entire world that keeps many people from becoming rich. The only cure is to simply stop it. But it's a lot harder to do than you may think. The only way to do it involves being able to activate your logical brain and remember your longer-term goals in the heat of a shopping moment.

Here's a little exercise that I discovered one time while shopping in the mall with my son. It takes just a minute to do, but reports back to me have been very positive. This technique has helped a lot of people, and if you struggle with impulse shopping or even just too much shopping, you may want to try it. Here's what happened with my son and me.

My son, Jared, at the time was thirteen years old. He set a goal in his logical brain that he wanted to save some money for a few things. One of them was to put money into a few investments that he had seen me get involved in. One investment involved buying shares in an income trust that paid out 12% annually in monthly dividends. That meant for every $1000 you invested with this fund, you could count on a monthly check of $10, and at the end of five or so years, you would also get your original $1000 back. I made Jared a deal that if he could come up with $500 I would match it to reach a total of $1000 for him to activate the investment. Jared was pretty excited about this opportunity and began saving.

A few months later we happened to be at the mall, and wouldn't you know it, we found the coolest snowboarding jacket ever. And of course, it was on sale. Jared was now coming close to $400 and the jacket was only $349. He turned to me and began to use his best teen-age begging skills to get me to loan him the money until we could get to the bank. It was then that this technique I am going to share with you came to mind.

Jared and I thought about how often he would actually wear the jacket. Since it was a winter jacket, and a specialized snowboarding jacket at that, we calculated that it might get worn maybe six or seven times that winter. Conclusion: seven.

Jared and I talked about how many years that jacket would fit him or be in style. He seemed to think probably three years, because he was expecting to grow. Conclusion: three.

That meant that he would realistically wear the jacket a total of twenty-one times before it would be passed on to a cousin or someone else. Jared could see where I was going and quickly did the math on his iPhone.

The cost of the jacket, $349.99, divided by twenty-one uses, and gave him a cost of $16.66 each time he wore the jacket. While that was accurate, I decided to remind him of the real value. And this is the point that I want to make. Most people, when they consider the cost of a purchase, look only at the price tag and do not consider the true value of the dollar in future terms.

This is how I did the math. Subtracting $349.99 from his $400 (which was almost $500) would leave him with $50.01. He would have to start his savings process almost from the beginning. At the rate which he accumulated the first $400, he would take another five months to return to where he was.

If he saved the money and continued to build it to the $500, I would match it so he would be up to $1000. The $1000 would then be placed in an investment which would return 12% annually and be paid out monthly over five years.

---

### POTENTIAL RETURN BY NOT BUYING THE JACKET

$500 + Dad's $500 = $1000
$1000 in the investment = $10/month
× 60 months (5 years) = $600

At the end of five years, the total value of his original $500 would have returned him $1,100.
Total future balance: $1,600
Price tag of the jacket: $349.99
Total times wearing the jacket: 21
Cost of owning the jacket: $1,600 ÷ 21 = $76.19 each time he wore the jacket

---

Jared decided to invest the money and buy the jacket at a future date. Now, I want to be clear. I am not suggesting that you never buy things you like. I am suggesting, with this technique, that you consider the future value of your money before you buy things that you could do without. There is an old saying that goes, "If you play now, you will pay later with interest. If you pay now, you get to play later with interest." Denying immediate gratification is an important element of growing and keeping your wealth.

I am happy to report that Jared has been very successful in learning this and at the moment of this writing, just before his fifteenth birthday he has $6550 in this particular income trust, is receiving checks every month for $65.50 and doesn't have to do anything to get them. The future looks very bright for him financially.

## A Side Note

By the way, there is another lesson that can be learned from this experience. Isn't it interesting that this opportunity for Jared appeared as he was so close to his goal? I have seen the same thing happen again and again in my life. Just when you are close to the finish line is when the biggest distractions appear. To get to your goal you will need to hang on and stay focused.

## Key Three: Expectations and Beliefs

We've all heard that what we expect and believe will happen usually does. Henry Ford once said it like this: "Whether you think you can or think you can't, you are right." I believe there is a lot of truth to this saying. But expectations and beliefs are also an essential area of wealth building that we don't hear very much about.

*Expectations and beliefs can only serve us if they are based on truth.*

Here's an example. Over the last decade, one of the most popular TV shows has been *American Idol*. We've all seen it at least a couple of times. Here's the example. Some kid, especially one of the weirder ones, begins to talk in a really overbearing manner about how they are destined to become the next American Idol. They pre-slam everyone and proclaim that they have already achieved so much and it is a gift to the world that they have decided to make this appearance today. The judges, they warn, are going to be blown away.

Then it's time to begin the audition. They open up their mouth to sing but we don't hear a beautiful noise. Instead, we hear bone-shattering, screechy tones that cause you to literally squirm in your chair. And the crazy part is that when one of the judges asks them how they think they did, they respond that they think they did well, sometimes even comparing themselves to musical greats like Mariah Carey, Beyoncé, Michael Jackson, Usher, Seal or others. I know you've seen those auditions. What were they thinking? How could they possibly believe they were destined to be the next big music superstar?

Here's the point: even though they believed with all their heart, they just didn't have the skills to pull it off. Because of their incorrect beliefs, they had never invested the time to find out if they were really on track. They never took the time to consider what they might have done to prepare better to possibly have a different outcome.

The same is true in the money world. Belief in your successful outcome is not enough. If you truly expect and believe in success, you also prepare.

*What you expect to happen, generally does. If you prepare.*

There are many incorrect expectations and beliefs about how money is made, what you should do once you have it and how it should be used to grow more.

### False Expectations Keep People From Success

One such funny example comes to mind from an event I recently spoke at. One of the attendees approached me just before I was to start speaking. I kind of wish I could have brought him on stage and shared the following interaction. I think it would have been helpful to many present.

He told me that he was looking forward to my presentation specifically because he felt that within that hour I would teach him all the keys skills of how to be rich. He felt that if I was really as good as what people, including the media, had been saying about me, then this hour was about to change his life.

I was flattered that he thought so much of my abilities. But his permanent financial success would take ongoing effort on his part. No one can make a person rich. And certainly not in an hour.

First false expectation: It takes more than an hour of time to understand how to become rich.

Second false expectation: I don't make anyone rich.

First true expectation: Becoming rich is a process that takes time and consistency.

Second true expectation: Creating your future wealth has very little to do with me. It really has everything to do with you.

After explaining this to him, I asked him a question to learn a little bit more about his thinking. The question might well be one I could ask you. And I would invite you to think about your answer. It will be instructive to you. The question was, "Why do you want to be rich?"

I have asked this question of many people over the years. The answer will always tell a lot about whether you will make it or not. More on this later. But here was his answer.

"I want to be a millionaire so I can go and live on the beach."

Wow. Let's be clear about what he meant. He further elaborated that his idea was basically a permanent vacation on the beach, without any cares or responsibilities. Okay, so here is a big problem that worried me. He thought my seminars would teach him how to live on the beach, with no responsibility and on a permanent vacation. Yikes. I don't live on a beach without responsibilities and I am not on a permanent vacation. I recognized I was unqualified to teach him what he wanted to learn.

As I began my career in personal development, I spent close to a decade interviewing and researching more than 400 of the world's top achievers. Almost everyone in the group was a millionaire, multi-millionaire or billionaire. In addition to that initial research group, I now have the opportunity to interact with hundreds of high net worth individuals every year. As a rough estimate, I have probably had interactions with more than 5 thousand millionaires in the last ten years. Out of that group how many do you think live on the beach?

Zero. Some of them have beach houses, but they are definitely not on permanent vacation.

I do know a few people who do spend most of their time hanging out on the beach in a vacation-like existence. Most of them operate businesses in the tourist industry. But they are not the millionaires.

False expectation: Money comes for free and I can be on permanent vacation.

True expectation: Although there are freedoms and opportunities that come with being a millionaire, there is also a degree of responsibility and effort required.

As you can see, false expectations can often derail us entirely from the possibility of success.

To discover your false expectations about wealth can sometimes be tricky. Much of them can be understood by just thinking about them on a slightly deeper level. In other words, really look at what you are expecting and see how that expectation matches in comparison to real life. Oftentimes just that simple exercise will help you spot the fairy tale from reality.

Sometimes it's a little more difficult. When you aren't sure about your expectation, study the lives of other millionaires and see how closely your expectation aligns with the reality of their lives. Does it seem like it would fit, or is it a little off target?

A great exercise that I use in my seminars is to have people write down the outcome they want and then list expectations of what they think it will take to get there. Together we look at cause-and-effect patterns among the wealthy. When these goals and expectations are put on paper and explored, it soon becomes apparent how incorrect they are. And by exploring the realties in the lives of the wealthy, patterns emerge that are effective in creating results.

One final thought about expectations. Imagine if you were hungry and wanted to go to a restaurant. Let's say you walked into a restaurant and ordered a meal. Less than a minute goes by, naturally you are still hungry, but the meal hasn't arrived. But you are also impatient. You want to eat now! Frustrated, you get up and go look for another restaurant.

You sit down and order another meal. Again thirty seconds passes and still no meal. You don't like being hungry. You want to eat now! Frustrated you get up and go find a third restaurant. You sit down and order a meal, and again thirty seconds passes by and no meal. You are so hungry! You want to eat now! You get up again and head to another restaurant.

Does this sound like a crazy story? It would actually be funny if so many people were not living their lives (especially their financial lives) this way.

Too often people get committed to a financial direction, they get started and then just like in the example, the results don't show up instantly. So what do they do? They shift gears to try something else.

I used to belong to a networking group in my city and there was a fellow who would come every week. About every three to four weeks he would come in with a new business card indicating a new service or product he was selling. It was no surprise that he was broke. It wasn't that the business ideas or products he represented were terrible. Many of those ideas were, in fact, very good. The problem was that he shifted gears to a new idea before any of these efforts gained traction. And as you can imagine, people became very nervous about doing business with him because they had no idea if the service or product they purchased from him would be around in another month. Here's the false expectation he had:

> False expectation: If something doesn't work right away, it must be wrong. Try something else.
> True expectation: Wealth building, like most of the more significant things in life, can take time.

Be very careful not to fall into this same trap. Wealth building, whether in business, investment or any other area, takes time.

*Don't get out of the boat before it reaches the shore.*

False expectations are a significant reason why some people are never able to build their wealth, and this typically comes down to false expectations about the correct actions required for success. Often, the worst incorrect expectations are the amount of effort and the time it will take to see results.

A bit of trivia: a high number of self-made millionaires today are made within three years of focused effort. Most are made in a long-term process of five years or more.

Your first million will be the most challenging. Your second one normally comes a lot more quickly than your first. But the time frame will really be up to you, based on two major factors:

1.  Method of growing the wealth
2.  Consistency and focus

## A Millionaire's Twist on Affirmations

Most people have heard of affirmations before. By definition, affirmations are positive or encouraging statements that we tell ourselves which give us hope, courage or a mind-set of success.

As I have talked about affirmations and shared them with people, I have been surprised to see many people begin by dismissing them as "new age" silliness, yet end up completely convinced that they were a primary reason for their financial increases.

Affirmations will shift your thinking. Scientific studies have demonstrated that affirmations work. In scientific terms they are not known as affirmations; instead, the psychological term *autosuggestion* is used as a description.

Here's how it works with our brain: autosuggestion triggers a specific chemical pathway between the neurons of the brain. As the autosuggestion is repeated, the pathway strengthens and the connection between those specific neurons is solidified.

Essentially, the neurons which regulate the way your thoughts flow and influence your beliefs in specific outcomes bring about your ability to create that outcome.[2] According to research, there are three components necessary for successful autosuggestion.

1. The affirmation must be stated in the present tense.
2. The affirmation must be positive in nature. (Negative ones work too, but we are trying to create positive results.)
3. The affirmation must be short and specific.

I have included some affirmations that are based on attributes and beliefs I have observed in millionaires I have worked with and studied over the last decade or so. I have shared both the attribute or the concept and then created an affirmation for you to begin to recite yourself. If you are interested in exploring the power of affirmations I encourage you to pick up my book and audio CD set *Millionaire Frequency*. That training material will put your mind in the right channel to start thinking more like a millionaire.

I encourage you not to pass over this activity. As I mentioned before, this is one activity that consistently surprises many of the people we work with. The results are quite remarkable. Take some time each day over the next thirty days to recite these affirmations to yourself and you will experience similar results.

Do not rush through them. Take time to say them with conviction, and really own them as part of who you are. (At the conclusion of this chapter there is a deeper exercise, called *affirm-actions*, which you can use to instill these ideas deeper into your mind-set.)

Attribute: Millionaires are possibility oriented.
Affirmation: I am possibility oriented.

Attribute: Millionaires have an abundant mind-set.
Affirmation: I have an abundant mind-set.

Attribute: Millionaires see what could be.
Affirmation: I am a person of possibility.

Attribute: Millionaires believe opportunities are always available.
Affirmation: Opportunities are flowing toward me constantly.

Attribute: Millionaires believe there is support and help when they need it.
Affirmation: Others around me want me to succeed.

Attribute: Millionaires believe it's okay to walk away from some deals.
Affirmation: There is always more coming. I choose the best.

Attribute: Millionaires believe in themselves.
Affirmation: I am more than enough. I deserve to be abundant now.

Attribute: Millionaires believe that they can solve challenges.
Affirmation: I have the resources and ability to solve any challenge.

Attribute: Millionaires believe in surrounding themselves with the best.
Affirmation: Everything and everyone around me is getting better and better.

Attribute: Millionaires believe they are worthy of being compensated.
Affirmation: My contributions are valuable and I deserve to be compensated.

Attribute: Millionaires believe in the importance of taking action.
Affirmation: I am proactive and make things happen.

Attribute: Millionaires believe they can change outcomes.
Affirmation: The future is in my hands. I make things happen.

Attribute: Millionaires believe money comes quickly and easily.
Affirmation: Money flows to me quickly and easily.

Attribute: Millionaires believe they are entitled to have more money.
Affirmation: The value I share brings me greater wealth.

Attribute: Millionaires believe they have already paid the price to be wealthy.
Affirmation: Wealth is flowing to me now. I have paid the price.

Attribute: Millionaires are on a constant quest of improvement.
Affirmation: I am finding opportunities everywhere to become better.

Attribute: Millionaires don't ask how much something costs, they look at the potential return.
Affirmation: I look for possibilities for progress and reward.

Several of these thoughts are based on affirmations in the program "The Millionaire Frequency," by Douglas Vermeeren, published by Ridley Jones, 2012. This program is a powerful tool for those who may be struggling with beliefs about money.

## EXERCISES

1. Clarity: Set some goals as to where you would like to be financially in the next six months, one year, five years and even ten years. Once you have an idea of where you want to be, spend some time working backward to identify what needs to be done along the way and determine the exact figures you will need to reach on a monthly, weekly, daily and even hourly basis.
2. Control the emotive brain: Naturally, it's easier to talk about than to do. It can take a lot of practice. One of the greatest things you can do is simply to be aware.

Keep a daily schedule that outlines your highest-priority activities, and if you miss an activity, go back and consider what it was that took you from that high-priority activity. If scheduled activities continue to fall by the wayside, consider whether that activity really has value or if it is just busy work.

You'd be surprised how often we fool ourselves into thinking that something is an important task when it doesn't really matter at all. And if it is important, try adding more powerful reasons behind *why* it needs to get done, and that activity will soon become a bigger priority.

3. Expectations: Begin carefully observing the patterns, behaviors and expectations of millionaires. What is it that they expect differently than what you expect and what the world in general expects?

4. Expectations: What are your expectations about what you will have to do in order to become financially abundant? Consider your current expectations and ask how realistic they are. How do they measure up against what you see in the lives of millionaires?

5. Create some of your own affirmations based on successful things you see self-made millionaires doing.

6. Here's an effective exercise I teach at some of the training sessions for The Millionaire Frequency program. Remember the list of affirmations that you read earlier in this chapter.

Affirmations have a lot of power to shift your thinking to be more powerful. But I find that too many people just stop there. They do not attach actions to these affirmations to bring them from thoughts into real life. It is for this reason I developed something called *affirm-actions*." Essentially, an affirm-action is an affirmation with an action attached.

For example, in the above list you read the affirmation: millionaires are possibility oriented. To make that statement an affirm-action you will now add to it an action that you will take right now to turn that concept into an activity in your life. You do this by adding the words, "So today I will …" and then filling in the blank with what action you will take.

Here's an example: "Millionaires are possibility oriented, *so today I will find a way to save an extra $100 in my monthly spending and invest it in something that will give me value back.*"

For this exercise I encourage you to go through each affirmation and come up with actions that you will do. The more frequently you do this, the more quickly your results will change. Pick five to ten affirmations and affirm-actions each day for the next month.

## QUESTIONS

1. What is my clear financial goal?
2. Why do I want this goal?
3. What will I do to stay connected to my logical goals when my emotional brain tries to take over?
4. What incorrect expectations do I have about wealth?
5. What will my life look like with more financial abundance?
6. What ideas do I need to adjust to be more realistic?
7. What are my expectations about the activities I will need to engage in to create more abundance in my life?
8. What expectations do I have about how much time it may take?
9. How much time does it take the average self-made millionaire to get there?
10. How can I speed up the process?
11. How do affirmations work?
12. Did I recite my affirmations today?
13. What affirm-actions can I include in my life today?

# What Will You Do to Start The Ball Rolling?

# Millionaire Habits

Have you ever driven down the road on automatic pilot and missed a turnoff that you needed because you are in the habit of driving past it? Or what about when you go to the shopping mall, is there a part of the lot that you always try to park in, even if other spots are available? What about when you are in the grocery store, is there a brand and style of bread that you always select regardless of how the others are priced and regardless of whatever other choices may be there for you?

These effects are all the result of habit. In psychology, these actions of habit are often referred to as ritual tendencies.

It is these ritual tendencies, the things which we do when we are on autopilot, that create the majority of the results in our lives. Often it is not the major, conscious actions that have the greatest influence on our lives, but rather these unconscious, automatic actions. According to recent research, more than 70% of our lives are spent in autopilot mode. That means that 70% of our energy day by day is spent doing the same kind of things we have always done, because these are the habits we have created.

Whether you are living a life of abundance or of lack, those results can all be traced back to your ritual tendencies and habits.

There are many ways to make money, but incorrect habits often keep us from getting involved with them.

## SO WHY DON'T WE CHANGE OUR HABITS?

If our habits dictate our results, why don't we just change our habits? We really only desire to change our habits for two reasons.

Reason one: We change when we encounter situations where our habits create stress or an uncomfortable situation that creates pain in our lives. When the results of our habits are not in our way, we don't think much about our habits at all.

For this reason, change is not always easy. It is not like a light switch that can be instantly turned on or off. Instead it is more like a dimmer switch that is turned gradually from darkness to light. We may take deliberate actions here and there, but true change and creation of habit is an ongoing process that requires a consistent effort in the beginning. However, the good news is that after a careful and consistent beginning, the new habits begin to take root. Once the new habits take root, the changes in your life will be exponential.

One of the most important first steps of creating new, successful habits is to be aware of what needs to change. Often, dramatic changes are not required to start seeing better results. It can simply be a matter of fine-tuning some little things that you are currently doing, eliminating a few of the things that aren't working in your life and then turning the volume way up on some of the things you may be doing well, but aren't necessarily doing enough of. Lasting changes are accomplished one step at a time.

If you can find the habits that you are doing well and expand those habits in your life, you will soon find that the successful habits will begin to crowd out the less successful habits. There is an old saying that when you focus and feed the best plants in the garden, the weeds will wither and die.

There is also a lot of truth to the 80/20 rule here. You've heard of the 80/20 rule? It's also known as the Pareto principle. Eighty percent of the positive results generally come from 20% of the best efforts. This rule is consistent through many aspects of productivity. Naturally, by applying this rule to yourself right now, it is very probable that you have 80% of your best results coming from 20% of your habits. Those habits you need to keep and improve upon. The other 80% of your habits right now are most likely the ones that are holding you back. Those are the ones that you need to replace with better ones. The key to increasing your wealth is constant improvement. Find ways to eliminate your weaker habits and strengthen and develop your stronger ones. Although the 80/20 rule is always going to be consistent, as you shift to stronger and stronger habits there will come a day when even your weakest habits in the future will be stronger than your strongest habits of today. At that time, even the weakest things you do will still give you better results than you are currently getting.

Are you aware of your habits? Most people aren't aware of their habits. Most people live in automatic pilot. Awareness is the key to change. The moment that you are aware that you are doing things out of habits that are not serving you is the minute that you can start making changes for your future.

Now, there is a second reason people's habits change. This one is vastly different, and the results are extraordinary. This is the reason that the most successful and extremely wealthy have discovered, and it is the most difficult to explain.

Reason two: Habits change when you live with purpose. I am not talking about setting a goal or having a mission statement. Living with purpose happens when we really decide and determine what we are here to do in our existence on earth. This discovery is an incredible thing. Some people call this finding your passion, but I think it's more than that.

When you live with purpose, everything you do shifts in your life to help you fulfill that purpose. Your habits will change without your thinking about them. You will wake up earlier to get to work on your ideas. You will attract the people to help you get there. You will reach further than you ever have before, and you will instinctively begin to know the answers as to what needs to be done.

Most people don't wake up in the morning and say, "Wow! That's it! I've discovered my purpose." It generally doesn't happen that way. In fact, most people take the same journey I did. They spend time in their lives making a few mistakes, first finding out what their purpose is not.

When I first came out of college, I worked at a telephone call center, then at an office supply store, then selling vacuum cleaners, then at a shoe store and the list goes on. My habits at the time were also undirected. I was not making much progress in my life and barely making ends meet. This went on for about a year or two. Then I got a job where I started to teach people and help them achieve their goals. It got me excited. This opportunity gave me the first glimpse of my spark. The more time I spent doing this teaching, the more the spark grew, until I began to recognize it as my purpose. It was then that I invested some time in really thinking about and considering what I was here on earth to do. And the more I thought about this spark, the more it grew into a flame. It became my purpose. Maybe it sounds a bit new-agey. Maybe it is.

This is still my core purpose today. Some people think it's to make money. It's not. It's to make a difference for other people. When you make a difference to other people, the money comes.

It kind of goes along with what Zig Ziglar, the great motivator and one of my heroes, said: "If you help enough people get what they want, you will soon get what you want."

If you want to become wealthy and also happy, the best way to do it is to discover your purpose and then throw your entire self into that purpose. When you do this your thinking, your habits and your results will all fall in line to help you fulfill that purpose.

Here are six habits that all self-made millionaires possess, and I invite you to consider how you can bring these concepts more fully into your life. To the degree that you can make them your own habits, you will see the financial situation in your life change for the better.

## Thinking Habits

How you think is a habit. Your thoughts are what determine your future. When we habitually think about failure or fear, that is what we create. We have all met someone who is focused on negative thoughts, and as a result they create situations where they become a victim. The truth is that what you think about most creates the patterns and results in your life.

The habits of our thoughts are much more consequential than we think. Most people don't really spend a lot of time thinking about their thoughts. Too often they just assume that a little thought doesn't carry much of a consequence.

Here's an interesting exercise that I believe teaches the importance of thinking empowering thoughts. For the next day, every time you have a thought that is not supportive or empowering, write it down boldly on a single piece of paper. This can include every thought of fear, discouragement, regret, doubt, frustration.

It is very easy to take one of the papers and rip it in half. But as the papers begin to stack up, it becomes harder and harder to tear through them. The same is true of our thinking.

The more we stack our negative thoughts together, the harder they are to rip through. Those thoughts become the strongest. They bind us and control our lives. The same can be said of the positive thoughts. When empowering thoughts are the dominant thinking, they become the strongest.

It is not just enough to think "I can do it," however. True success comes when your thoughts are even more fine-tuned to your positive financial goals. The more you focus on being a better money thinker, the more your results will grow into positive results.

## A Difference Between Broke and Poor

As I discussed earlier, there is a difference between broke and poor, and it all comes down to your thinking. *Broke* is a temporary situation where you find yourself without enough money. *Poor* is a state of mind where you cannot see hope that your situation will change. Broke is fixable. Poor is not.

## Education Habits

What you earn will be a reflection of what you learn. Learning is a major habit that all high net worth individuals develop. As you learn more about wealth strategies, you will gain more power to participate in wealth opportunities. You can only get involved in opportunities that you become aware of. Education creates that awareness.

The world around us is always changing. Especially the financial world. If you want to be highly successful, you need to be aware of what tools are available to you.

One of the challenges that most people experience when it comes to building wealth is that they do not know what they don't know. They don't know what opportunities they are missing out on because they are not aware of what opportunities might be available to them.

As you develop your education, you will grow in your ability to evaluate opportunities that come your way. While there are no guarantees in the investment or business worlds, your chances for success increase dramatically as you gain education that allows you to more effectively evaluate opportunities that come your way.

Education is mandatory if you want to become successful in wealth building.

## Spending Habits

How you spend your money can make all the difference to your future financial success. Too often people don't think carefully about the purchases they make, and as a result they end up broke. When you live with purpose like I described above, your money and energy naturally get consumed by what your purpose is. But most people have to work very hard to control their spending in the beginning, before the spark of purpose reveals itself.

Your financial success will not start with you having a lot of money. Instead, it will develop as you learn to spend what you have in more effective ways.

Remember that every purchase you make is an investment. At the beginning of the book we talked about QCC (Quality of life, Create and Contribute). You are trading your money for what you value most. The challenge most people experience is that they value immediate gratification in their quality of life more than they value future financial freedom. Financial freedom comes only as we create.

Here's the most deceiving part of this equation. Most people don't realize that if they exercise a little self-control for a period of time, they can soon have both the immediate gratification and the financial freedom.

*Play now, pay later, with interest.*

When spending is not controlled at the beginning of the journey, freedom and opportunity are lost further down the road.

It is important to remember that every purchase you make is an investment in your future. It is almost as though you are buying a ticket to what your future will look like. If you are wise in the present, your future will open up to you in the most positive ways. You are always trading your money for what you value most in the moment. If you make a habit of trading your money for things that increase in value or to create (even the little stuff), you will notice a remarkable shift in your net worth.

**To Save or Not to Save?**

A note on saving: while saving is far more beneficial than spending money aimlessly, it is also not the goal. Keeping your money in a savings account does not create exponential growth. You need to do more with your money than just let it sit. When I say "don't save your money" at seminars, I always get people who look at me with confusion. They start asking questions like, "Shouldn't I have cash on hand?" and "What if I am trying to put together money for a big investment or a real estate deal?" or "Shouldn't I keep cash on hand in case of an emergency?"

The answer to all of those questions is yes. But don't keep that money in a savings account. There are many opportunities to have your money in a secure situation and still have it accessible to you. It's just that a savings account isn't the best place.

There are many better opportunities that will pay you more than the typical interest—which can be anywhere from .05 to .15%—paid by a bank on a savings account. Here are some options that will generally keep your cash secure, keep it relatively accessible and pay a higher rate of return:

- Money market accounts
- Money market mutual funds
- Online savings accounts
- Treasuries
- Mutual fund accounts
- Microloans
- Savings bonds
- Certificates of deposit
- Selected stocks

I invite you to do a little research to find which of these may work best for you. Many organizations offer these opportunities and returns, and fees may vary. A good place to start is simply to Google "better options than the bank." You will be surprised what options come up.

**Work and Service Habits**

Have you seen a pendulum before? A pendulum is simply a weight attached to the bottom of a string. It can be used to demonstrate a simple principle of physics. The principle is that the movement of the pendulum along its arc is in proportion to the force placed upon it. The greater the force against the pendulum, the higher the pendulum will rise along its arc and the longer it will stay in motion.

There is also a pendulum in the laws of creating wealth. What sets the pendulum in motion is simple. The principles that activate the pendulum's motion are simple: work and service.

**Work**

You'll notice I didn't say *hard work*. I don't believe that wealth is created exclusively by hard work. There are many people in the world who work very hard. In fact, in many third world countries, people are working very hard every day just to maintain survival. According to reports published on income levels around the world, some of these individuals are grossing an income of under $100 US per year. Hard work does not necessary equal a life of ease.

A person does not get paid based on how hard they work. They are compensated based on the level of problems they solve or the value they bring to others. Now having said that, work is a component of either solving those problems or bringing value to others. I believe work done in the right way is rewarded. But the work must be performed doing the right things.

Wealth is never built by accident. It requires deliberate, focused commitment.

### Service and Solutions

Wealth is grown in proportion to the value of your service or the problems you solve. Growing wealth always involves two people. One to give the money and one to receive the money. It's pretty simple. People are only willing to give you money if you provide a valuable service to them or solve their problems. If you are fortunate enough to receive money from someone, and you have not been successful doing one of these two things, chances are very high that they will not give you money again. Service and solutions will always precede financial success.

*Wealth, like happiness, is never attained when sought after directly. It comes as a by-product of providing a useful service.*
—Henry Ford

Your bank statement is your report card on how well you give service or provide solutions.

*Solution and service = Your financial success*

A few considerations in providing service and solutions:

Who are you serving?
Are you offering the right things they need to solve their problems and be of high service to them?
Have you structured a way to be compensated for your service?
How can you package your service?

## You Don't Have to Service Everyone to be Successful

This is perhaps one of the biggest mistakes that most entrepreneurs make when they launch a new business or idea. They feel that the only way to make a lot of money is to service and sell to everyone. The irony of this is that the really big money in business is found in more precise targeting. And what may be most surprising is that the target doesn't have to be a large group. Serve those with whom your mission resonates most, and they will reward you for it.

*The aim of marketing is to know and understand the customer so well the product or service fits him and sells itself.*
—Peter Drucker

## Don't Forget to Get Paid

Just a word of caution about something that I have seen happen to enthusiastic entrepreneurs again and again. When you build your enterprise in an area that you love, it is very easy to attract others who will love what you do. Your customers will become your friends. As they become your friends, it will feel difficult at times to charge them for your services. It's nice to be appreciated for what you do, but without a financial expression of gratitude from your customers, you cannot build your wealth or stay in business.

*A business absolutely devoted to service will have only one*
*worry about profits. They will be embarrassingly large.*
—Henry Ford

## How are You Serving?

This is perhaps the single most important aspect of service and work. If you want to be highly successful, you have got to be considered by your customers as the best option for them in terms of what you are offering. Trying to beat your competitors on pricing rarely works in trying to create massive financial success.

Instead, you have got to establish a reputation of being elite—one of the best—and an expert in every way. Especially if your specific clientele is also the wealthy elite. They want the best in everything. If you are the best, you have a right to be expensive. If you are second best, you must automatically find other ways (which can include lowering your pricing) to attract customers.

## Top Customers Find the Best Services

When I was about sixteen I had a conversation with the father of one of my friends. He was very financially successful compared with my family. So I asked him one day the secret to becoming rich. His answer was simple: "Find something you love. Become the best at it. Then people will come and find you and pay you for what you do." Becoming the best at a specific thing is important if you want to stand out in the eyes of your customers.

Your best customers are also on a quest to find the best and become the best. If you fit in with that quest, you become part of their essentials.

## A Note on What You Choose

It is not enough to simply find something to become the best at. I have said this before, and it must be said again: you need to find a relevant problem to solve or deliver high value for your potential clients. The best option is for you to begin by putting yourself in their shoes and consider problems that they need to solve, and then become the go-to person for that solution. The greater the headache or challenge you solve, the more you will be compensated.

What is a big problem that your customers have? How can you solve it for them in a way that makes sense for them to hire you, and how much is the solution worth to them?

*You can start right where you stand and apply the habit of going the extra mile by rendering more service and better service than you are now being paid for.*
—Napoleon Hill

## Systems Habits

When it comes to building wealth, having systems in place is crucial. Systems are procedures that are put in place for the delivery of your service to your clients and for how you get paid for it. To be effective, systems must be able to be duplicated repeatedly. To have an effective system, you must be able to step away and have the system continue without your constant, direct involvement. The most effective systems also provide ways for you to measure their effectiveness at any time.

## Systems Allow You to Expand

With a system in place, you can expand and grow. One of the most important factors that is required for growth is the ability to duplicate yourself. You do this by adding other people to your business or venture. The only way to do this effectively is to have a system. Adding new people requires that they contribute to your mission and become effective in offering more of what is currently making you money. If a person cannot fit into your system and contribute, they will be slowing you down. It has been said that it is easier to run with a hundred people going in the same direction as you, than it is to run against one who is trying to hold you back.

A great example of a system that works is the McDonald's company. Wherever you go in the world, McDonald's is the same. Everything is the same from the way the restaurants look to the way they operate inside. I have been to McDonald's from China all the way to France, Germany, Canada and the United States. They are more or less identical. It's because McDonald's has a great system.

Generally, if a McDonald's unit has a problem it can be traced to someone not sticking with the program. And if you stray too far off the program, you will be replaced.

### Systems Allow You to Sell Should You Ever Want to

When I was in high school, there were several T-shirt companies that were quite successful. One of those brands was a company called No Fear. They had catchphrases and artwork that was aimed at inspiring people to live on the edge. Growing up I was involved in martial arts, and seeing the success of the No Fear brand, I thought I could get involved in the T-shirt business.

I called my company Intensity. I started by making T-shirts specifically for martial arts tournaments, and almost immediately my designs became popular. It wasn't long until other organizations outside of the martial arts community began to approach me to have T-shirts created for their events. As my company grew, an interesting thing happened. I was approached by a large company interested in buying my little company. They started talking about quite a bit of money. This immediately got my attention.

Our negotiations, however, did not last long as they soon found out I didn't have any real systems. Everything that my company did was directly attached to me and my designs. Even the way that I was connecting with the martial arts community was all word of mouth. As the big company withdrew their offer to buy my company, I was told something that has stayed with me ever since: "The reason why we can't buy your company is that it has no systems we can duplicate. No systems means no growth."

Unless others could duplicate what I was doing there was no value in my company to anyone else. That was a powerful lesson.

## Simplicity is The Key to System Success

As a rule, the more complex a system is, the more difficult it is to implement. Successful systems should be easy to implement, regulate, manage and teach to others. Generally speaking, the more complex a system is, the more costly it is to implement and manage. But here's the problem with simplicity. Was it Socrates who said, "The most complex thing is to find simplicity?" Your system will require consistent refinement to become simple.

## A Note on Systems and Investing

Too often people struggle to make the shift from business income to investment income because of one simple thing. They invest only when they feel that they have enough money set aside to make it worthwhile. The truth is, investing even a few hundred dollars consistently can make a huge difference in your overall financial future over a short period of time. The key to growing wealth through investment isn't necessarily the amount of money you invest; the key is found in consistency.

Consistency can also be created by implementing a system. Many investment opportunities let you set up an automatic transfer of funds directly from your bank account into their offering or program. By setting one of these systems up you won't miss the money, but you will be very surprised at how quickly your investments begin to grow.

## Effective Relationship- and Network-Building Habits

This habit is so important I have written a separate book—*Network Like a Millionaire*—on the importance of building relationships and networking when it comes to growing wealth.

The reason why this habit is so important is that wealth is a team sport. It cannot be created by one individual. Your wealth grows in proportion to the number and quality of people you have involved in your wealth-building process.

It starts with the relationship between you and a single customer. You cannot make any money without having someone else who will give it to you. Beyond that, you will grow exponentially as you find more people to give you money and perhaps members of your team who can help you collect it.

Networks also include having people to share ideas with you on what to do with your money. While many of my personal opportunities come from businesses or organizations that I have tracked down through the Internet or the Yellow Pages, the bulk of my really big opportunities have come through my immediate network.

These big opportunities have all come to me because of my relationships with people. Oftentimes in these relationships, I have been able to find out about opportunities long before they were made available to the public. Many of these opportunities never went public.

If you go to my Web site, you'll notice that I get invited to a lot of parties and VIP events. In fact, recently I was at a private event with Oprah Winfrey. Those kinds of invites don't happen by accident. They happen because of relationships in my network. Making your life a millionaire experience is only partly about having the money. To have a lifestyle at a millionaire level you also must have the relationships.

Here are a few thoughts on relationships and networks that I believe are worth noting. To explain these concepts, I'd like to use the words *relationship* and *network* separately.

Let's break the word *relationship* into two parts: *relation* and *ship*.

Relation: All your relationships are not equal. You will have to understand and assign them value in relation to each other. All business relationships have different value, and you will have to determine where to best spend your time. It is also important to realize that while one relationship may be valuable today and another not, this may change in the future. No relationship is static; they are always in motion. It will be important for you to monitor and nurture your relationships regularly.

Ship: Sometimes when people describe negotiations or business relationships, they suggest the idea of trying to achieve a win/win for all involved. While I do believe a win/win is important, I like to look at it a little differently. I like to use the analogy of "we are all in the same boat in a journey." That's the connection to the word *ship*. We are all in the same boat and probably will be for a long time. We are in the same boat in two ways. Firstly, we all have needs, wants, objectives and desires. That's the destination where the boat needs to go. When you can understand how to help satisfy those conditions or the destination for another person, they are prepared to help you obtain your own conditions and destinations. If they happen to be the same, the boat will get there faster and more effectively. But even if they aren't identical, recognizing destinations can go a long way toward moving the boat along. In that way we are alike and in the same boat.

Secondly, we are in the same boat for a specific length of time. You can't easily or too quickly get out. What I mean by that is that most often in your particular field or industry you will continually encounter those you network with, and have the possibility for continued business. In this sense you are in the same boat for an extended length of time. Because your association will be lengthy, you must treat those in your networks in ways that will be positive. Remember to be professional and courteous to all. As I mentioned above, all relationships are in motion. There is no such thing as a static relationship. Someone you may not get along with today may out of necessity become a partner in the future. There's nothing worse than burning a bridge and needing to cross it later.

I'd like to do the same with the word *network—net* and *work*.

Net: One of the things that I enjoy in my relationships with people in my network is that on occasion, they have actually acted as a safety net for me. They have given me advice, helped me avoid mistakes, and in some cases, helped me complete a deal that otherwise I would not have been able to do. If you are there for people in your networks, often they will be there for you.

Work: Building and maintaining these relationships can take work. You will need to invest time and effort to nurture these relationships. Any relationship that is all take and no give soon withers and dies.

## EXERCISES

1. Take a look at your money habits from the last week. How have you spent your money recently? How have you saved or invested?

2. Consider what habits you currently have that are serving you well. How can you turn up the volume and start doing more of those things in your life right now?

3. What are your current dominant thoughts about wealth? Are your current thoughts giving you power or taking it away?

4. Look for and take advantage of financial education opportunities around you. Set a goal to read at least one new book on financial strategy and attend one course in the next month.

5. Take the last thirty days of your life. Where have you been spending your money? It might be useful to remember what we talked about at the beginning of the book when we divided purchases into Quality of life, Create and Contribute. Remember that the category of Create is generally where your increase in financial abundance can be found. Where have you been spending your money?

6. What systems do I have in place right now to assist in growing my wealth? How could I improve on these systems right

now? How can I simplify them? What aspects of my system are costing me time and money?

7. Set up an automatic funds transfer for an investment opportunity. Remember, the amount of money doesn't have to be large. It is more important to be consistent. Do this today!

8. One of the tools that we use in our office to determine which relationships to spend the most time on is called the relationship radar. Essentially it works like this: On the wall I have a giant bullseye image, with a small center circle expanding into ever larger circles. At the heart is where I put my most important contacts. These are the ones that I need to dedicate the most effort and time to developing. These are the people who are generating the most significant results in my life right now and that I want to expand my relationship with. As the circle expands outward on this chart, I include people who are important to me but are worthy of less and less of my attention. I write the name and contact information of each contact on a card (or use their business card) that can be moved within the circles of the radar. This has been very helpful in reminding me who my most valuable contacts at any given time are.

## QUESTIONS

1. What are the habits that are keeping you from increased wealth?
2. What habits are actually working for you right now that you can do more of?
3. What new habits do you need to create for success?
4. What thoughts are currently giving you more financial power? How can you develop more of this kind of thinking?
5. Are you broke or poor?
6. How are you currently increasing your financial education?
7. How are you currently spending your money?

8. How are these purchases contributing to the future that you want?
9. What can you be doing better?
10. Who are you serving?
11. Can they support what you are offering?
12. Are you offering the right thing they need to solve their problems? Can you be of high service to them?
13. Have you structured a way to be compensated for your service?
14. How can you package your services?
15. What problems are there right now that need to be solved?
16. What problems are keeping you from being your best?
17. What problems keep recurring?
18. What value are you exchanging for your current income?
19. How can you give more value?
20. How can you provide value elsewhere that would compensate you?
21. What systems do you have in place in your wealth strategies right now?
22. How are you able to recruit and train other people to help you within this system?
23. What relationships are bringing you most of your results?
24. What relationships are you dedicating time to that are slowing you down?

# How Money Comes to You

MONEY IS IMPORTANT TO everyone on the planet. Places to go where you don't need money are virtually non-existent. The rates at which it comes and how it arrives may be very different, but arrive it must. That's what this chapter is about.

Once you recognize how money arrives, you can begin to direct more of the roads that money is traveling on toward you.

Money arrives primarily in two main ways. These ways are known as events and streams. Let's talk about each one.

## EVENTS

*Events* are specific one-time activities that bring money into your life. Typically events are tied to large sums of money. Examples of events are the sale of real estate, the reception of an inheritance, a significant commission on a big deal and even winning the lottery. Typically events don't occur regularly and cannot be counted on as a recurring contributor to your financial situation. Events often take time to orchestrate, and sometimes they can't be counted on at all. Deals fall through, real estate sales don't always return what you'd expect and your chances of winning a lottery are extremely thin. Having said this about events, I would still encourage you to develop them around you. The better you get at constructing events, the more of them you will have happen in your financial career.

## STREAMS

*Streams* are the more common way money will flow into your life. There are typically two kinds of streams that bring money flowing into your life.

### Linear Income Streams

The most common kind of stream is known as a *linear stream* of cash flow. Most people participate in this form of revenue stream. Essentially, a linear stream is where you trade a portion of your time for a specified amount of money. The most common example is working a given number of hours each week in exchange for a paycheck, but there are many other sources of linear income.

You may be thinking to yourself, wait a minute. I have heard that rich people don't trade their time for money. That concept is only partially true. While the rich have other income streams, which we will talk about in a moment, they still participate in linear income streams. Consider this for a just minute: when Bill Clinton is hired to speak, he is reportedly paid $160 thousand for his hour, not to mention travel and other expenses. Is that not trading time for money? Even though the amount is staggering, it is indeed a linear income pattern. Or what about when the owner of a company has a meeting with his management team or CEO? He may not get a piece of paper detailing what he was paid for his three hours with them, but the money he is benefiting from is tied to his ability to direct and lead his team. Wherever time is required, even if it's only a small amount, a linear pattern exists. Everyone benefits from linear income to some degree.

To grow your wealth does not require you to eliminate linear income streams. Instead, it becomes your duty to increase the productivity of your linear income stream.

Productivity isn't defined as doing more. In other words, I am not suggesting that you need to go out and spend more time in your linear income stream. Quite the contrary. Productivity is the measurement of the gap between your efforts and your results. I want you to learn how to do less but achieve more. That is an increase in productivity. So in other words, what can you improve? Spend less time but create bigger results. Make more effective use of your time to get increased financial rewards.

For many people, their current linear stream is a full- or part-time job. While this linear stream does provide cash flow to you, it is the least productive kind of linear stream.

Perhaps when people are saying they don't want to trade their time for money, what they are really saying is they don't want a job. A job is not the best form of a linear income stream. This is true is because when you are working for someone else, your linear income stream has a limit and specific parameters as to how you can use that time to grow income. You lose a certain amount of control.

When you control your linear income streams, you get to determine how much money your time represents, and you can constantly improve productivity in that time. When you work for someone else, they dictate these factors.

### Should I Quit My Job?

The question of should I quit my job or when should I quit my job is one that you will have to decide. We will talk more about this in the next chapter. But for now, I will share some great wisdom my father shared with me. He advised me to never quit my current job until I had something better to replace it with.

### Passive Income Streams

If linear income streams can identified by the involvement of time, passive income streams are identified by the lack of time required to operate them. Massive wealth is grown by creating passive income streams. Naturally, all passive income streams require an initial investment of time to set up, but once they are up and running they require no babysitting.

In the previous chapter we talked about the habit of creating systems. Systems are essential when it comes to creating passive income streams. The income that will arrive to you by systems can be created either through your efforts or by the efforts of someone else. In other words, you will make passive income through your own business system activities or by investing in the systems of someone else.

## Multiple Income Streams Versus Multiple Passive Income Streams

One of the things that I hear frequently is the idea that it is important to create multiple income streams. While I don't have a problem with the idea of having money coming in from various sources, I want to caution you against being too attached to the term *multiple income streams*. Why? you may ask. Well, simply because it's missing the word *passive*. Many people work several part-time jobs to create multiple income streams. They have a job before their job, another one after their job and maybe even another one after that.

When I was in my late teens, before college, I operated like that for a while. I did a paper route in the early hours of the morning, went to my full-time job during the day and then a part-time job in the evening. I had multiple income sources. But it was unsustainable; I was on the edge of exhaustion. It also didn't really give me the lifestyle I wanted. Wealth isn't just about making money, it's about enjoying it, too.

Multiple income streams are good to aim for, just try to create them as passive income streams.

## Begin With One And Do It Right

One of the common challenges I see many people encounter when they are building passive income streams is that they begin to create a second passive income stream before the first one is running successfully. Take the time to set up each passive income stream effectively. Once it is established correctly, you can then step away to successfully build others. A great way to do this quickly is to get involved with investments that already have a structure in place.

## Use Your Passive Income to Feed More Passive Income

The quickest way to grow wealth is to feed your passive income streams. In other words, as your passive income streams generate you an income you should endeavor to use that money to create or expand more passive income streams in your life. Too often when people begin making money through their passive income streams, they think of the additional money as a bonus that they need to go out and spend. Exponential growth is not made by spending those returns. It is made my multiplying them. You multiply them by directing this additional money to create new investments or streams of income.

## Should I Ever Shift, Replace or Close Down Passive Income Streams?

Every once in a while I get asked a really good question at the seminars that I teach, one that I hadn't really fully considered before, but that is very relevant to the pattern of wealth growth. This was such a question: should I ever shift, replace or close down a passive income stream?

Building passive income streams is only part of the mission. Where the real success comes is in monitoring them, improving them and, quite frankly, replacing them when necessary.

Although the question at the seminar did come out of the blue, I realized that in the past I had done all of the above. I have shifted, replaced and, quite frequently, closed down passive income streams. There is an appropriate time to do each of the above. Here are the criteria with which I have made decisions in the past to shift, replace or close down a passive income stream.

## The Stream Stops Producing or Starts Costing You Money

If the income stream stops producing, by all means shut it down. Especially if it starts costing you money. You don't want to have commitments that cost you money just because at one time they brought you an income. Sometimes this can be really tough, especially if you created the stream personally from the beginning. It has figuratively become a part of you, and you may be emotionally attached to it. But go it must. You cannot be emotionally tied to the activity. You've got to remember why it was created in the first place. If you become emotionally attached, this will impair your judgment on the matter and cost you money.

Every once in a while an investment opportunity has come into my life that I am interested in on a much deeper level than money. And I have to confess that on a few of these occasions I have let my emotions dictate my activities more than I should have.

Here's one example. The first week, I invested $10 thousand because I really liked the idea. Within a few weeks the investment went up to just over $14 thousand. It was exciting. Something that I loved was already giving such a good return. I decided to invest more. I put in another $30 thousand.

The investment went up again. Now I was sitting at just over $50 thousand. Not bad for a few weeks. I was up more than $10 thousand. I decided to put another $20 thousand into the program.

All of sudden, things changed. In the next week I lost about $5 thousand. Not so bad considering I was ahead by so much. The next week I lost another $7 thousand. Part of me, the logical part of me, felt like it was time to get out. At least I'd have all the original money I put in and a few bucks to spare.

As I mentioned, at the beginning of this investment I was really excited emotionally about it, so at this point I decided to stick with it, although everything logical told me it was best to get out now.

Over the next two weeks I lost an additional $45 thousand. I was now upside down in this investment. But did I get out? No. Again I was emotionally charged about this investment and I stuck around. Naturally, it went back down again. I still own the shares.

It'll actually cost me more to try to sell them than what I'd probably make out of the deal. Will these shares ever come back up in value? Who's to say? But the point I want to make, and the point that I live by now, is to make better decisions by trying to keep the emotion out of it.

### The Stream Starts Requiring Effort

If the passive income stream starts demanding time and effort, it is no longer a passive income stream. It has now become a linear income stream. Sometimes this kind of income stream can be redirected and repositioned as a passive income stream by systematizing it or restructuring how money is generated with it. Sometimes, this now linear stream does not take a significant effort, but does require some. You will have to decide the scale of the burden it is going to create for you. But my goal when an income stream shifts to linear is to try and get it back on track to be passive as quickly as possible. If this happens with too many of your income streams, you have just found yourself with a series of part-time jobs. Just as with other part-time jobs, you can only do so much effectively in your life. If the work load becomes overwhelming, the success of these income streams will suffer.

### Better Options Appear

Sometimes in the course of your quest for financial abundance, you will encounter better passive income opportunities that were perhaps not accessible to you before or of which you simply weren't aware when you created your initial passive income streams. At times like this, it may be valuable for you to shift your existing efforts into the new possibilities. This will be a choice that you will have to consider as you weigh your options.

## Finding Really Good Passive Income Streams

One of the excuses that people sometimes use to explain why they are not engaged in passive income streams is that they don't know where to find them. In the last few chapters we talked directly about where to find and how to evaluate good investment opportunities, which are passive income streams when they are correctly functioning. But what about finding business-style passive income streams? Business income streams differ from other passive income streams as they are attached directly to businesses you may own or operate. Where will you find opportunities like this?

There are many good locations to find these passive business income streams, but there are also many that look good on the surface but don't really produce stellar results. Sometimes the crummy ones are very difficult to discover because those who build them are very skilled at making them look like the successful ones.

When I am hosting events, without exception I am asked about the following two business models for creating an income stream. One of them is passive, while the other one, I feel, is more linear, although some people think it too is passive.

### Internet-Based Business

There are a lot of Internet businesses claiming that they can make you a ton of money in a very short period of time. Some of these genuinely work very well, yet others don't work at all.

A few things to consider when opening an online business:

- Avoid paying excessive fees to get started.
- Consider the kind of support you will get to start.
- Consider the product or service that is offered.
- Connect with others already involved in the program to explore their results.
- Ask about the method of payment to you.

## Network Marketing Companies

It has been suggested that network marketing as a whole has produced more millionaires than any other business model in the history of the world. I believe that network marketing can be a powerful tool for creating wealth, in addition to training people to think and act with greater abundance. The personal development training offered by many of these network marketing companies is alone almost worth participation. But having said this, not all network marketing companies are created equally, and there are dangers to be aware of.

A few things to consider when working with a networking marketing company:

- Although almost all of them will tell you that you are creating your own business, the truth is that your business is ultimately tied to their business. If their business disappears, often your entire support system will go with it. You will have no way of supplying your customers.
- Recent statistics have revealed that a high percentage of new start-up network marketing companies last only three to five years in the marketplace. It would be a shame to put extensive time and effort into building a strong business in a company that disappears just as you become successful.
- Look for longevity and a company with a proven track record.

## Is Network Marketing a True Passive Income Stream?

Is network marketing a true passive income stream? I am not sure that it is, although it can closely resemble one. Now I want to be clear that I am not saying this is a poor choice for an income stream. Again, this system has made more millionaires than any other business model, and often did it in a very short period of time, too. But I do want to manage your expectations.

Passive income means that once the initial system is set up, very little work is required on your part to be successful. The system more or less runs itself. Some networking marketing systems can be a little different. You may be required to continue investing significant time and effort growing and maintaining a team beneath you. You may also have a requirement of paying monthly fees to maintain your business. Some companies also require the monthly purchase of products.

If you stop participating in the company's requirements, your income may diminish or stop. In some ways, a network marketing business is more similar to a linear stream.

Again, this is not bad, but if the network marketing company you choose has involvement requirements, you will need to be highly productive in order to build great wealth using this system.

### Avoid Paying Expensive Fees to Get Started and Continue In The Program

Nearly all network marketing companies have fees to begin the business and ongoing fees to maintain the business. Naturally, your goal in becoming involved is to have your efforts reward you financially. If the fees are extensive then it will be harder for you to make a profit.

### Consider The Kind of Support You Will Receive

One of the most important things in building a network marketing business is having the support that you will need to be successful. If you have a great support network, you can accomplish incredible things. If you don't, it will be very tough to get far. Your support network doesn't just include those who are immediately supervising your efforts; it also includes those involved in your head office, those who ship the products to you and those who help you manage your team. Look for a group that has a proven track record in these areas and is prepared and excited to see your success.

### Consider The Product or Service That Is offered

This is in an important consideration, especially in the wake of the recession that we have just experienced and are still feeling the aftershocks of. One of the big challenges a lot of network marketing companies experienced was directly related to the lack of value compared to the cost of their products. While many of these products did great while the economy flourished, the minute money became tight they were discarded for things that were necessary for survival. When evaluating a product line to take on, consider carefully how much of a necessity and how fairly priced it is. The higher the value the product provides, the more likely it will stay important to your clients.

### How Easy is it to Get Others Involved?

Growth of your organization is a key to financial growth in network marketing. So attracting and involving people becomes an important issue.

How easy is it for others to get involved? It not only needs to be affordable, but it needs to be easy to do. Each step toward participation becomes a barrier to inclusion. If it gets too complex, most people won't even bother.

### Connect With Others Already Involved in The Program to Explore Their Results

If network marketing is the business model you decide to pursue, the best way to gauge if a program is a good fit for you is to meet with the network's existing members. By seeing what the results look like in real life, you can make a more informed decision and approach the company with both eyes open.

When you are connecting with members, look carefully at those who have had positive experiences as well as those who have had negative experiences. And no matter what anyone tells you, there will always be someone who has had a negative experience.

Naturally, I would invite you to be cautious when listening to both sides. Network marketing tends to polarize people. They either love it or hate it. Try to make judgments based on realities, not opinions.

## How Will You Get Paid?

In network marketing it is important to understand compensation structures and also methods and frequency of payment.

As you will be trading your effort for compensation, you want to spend some time making sure you understand how you will get paid. Remember, getting paid frequently for productive effort is your goal.

Below are a few traditional income streams that I have found great success with.

## Loans or Microloans

When you have money, you can make more by lending it out. This is the way that banks make a significant amount of money. They do it in the form of credit lines, business loans, mortgages and credit card loans. But you don't have to be a bank to participate in loans like this. To become a lender there are a few things you need to keep in mind.

## To whom do I Lend?

Many of the payday loan–type organizations focus on lending to just about anyone who can show proof of a paycheck. For the average lender this can be a bit risky. You don't have an infrastructure in place when it comes to processing and collecting on debts that may go bad. In my lending practices I don't lend to high-risk individuals. Instead I focus on more secure professional groups. I either lend to low-risk individuals or businesses. We'll talk a little bit more below about what I mean by low risk.

## Rates

Lending rates vary from location to location. In my geographical location, payday style–loans lend out money at a rate of $23 per $100 lent out over fourteen days. Naturally, additional penalties can be built into the agreement when payments are late or missed. You can often find the lending rates for your area online.

## License

Most states and provinces require a lender license, although there are a lot of people who do it without a license. While you can lend privately to individuals you know or have a relationship with, a license is required to engage in lending to the general public. In my area, the cost of a license is $25 thousand.

## Agreements

You need to have good agreements. If you don't have a good agreement, your borrower may not ever have to pay you back. It is worthwhile to have a lawyer create or review any agreement you determine to use.

## Security

As a rule, there needs to be security for any loan you make. You will have to decide what that level of security looks like to have you feel comfortable. In my own efforts, I try to always have a 5:1 ratio for lending. In other words, the borrower needs to demonstrate five times the security for the money I am lending. I also require that the items being put up for security can easily be turned into liquid cash.

## Collection Methods

Collection agencies can pursue debtors for you. They often charge between 30% and 40% for their efforts. I always include in my agreements that if the account is sent to collections, the borrower is responsible for the collection fees.

In a worst-case scenario, the debt may also go to small-claims court or litigation. I also am sure to include in my agreement that the borrower is responsible for all such costs. In fact, I specify that there will be a minimum of $1,500 immediately tacked onto their bill if I have to go this route. I have never had to go this route, and I believe these large price tags have been a part of the reason why.

## Rent to Own

This is a great strategy to use in a depressed real estate market. Generally when people think of real estate, they immediately think of buying a property and either renting it out or fixing it up and "flipping it" for a profit. While both those strategies are profitable, there is one strategy that you don't hear very often but that I like a lot.

In a depressed market there are still many people who would like to buy a home. Unfortunately with all kinds of homes foreclosing everywhere across the nation, the banks are becoming more cautious about their lending practices. But people still want to get into houses as owners rather than renters.

## No Manager

Here's a big benefit that makes this a passive income opportunity. When you simply rent a property to someone, you become the manager. If something goes wrong with a toilet or a furnace, either you or someone you hire has to go out and fix it. Owning a rental property can be a big babysitting job. This is one of the most significant reasons many people don't get into buying and renting property.

But when you use this rent-to-own strategy, the occupant becomes their own manager. They have a vested interest in the property and as a result they take care of it. Naturally, in the agreement, the title doesn't shift to the tenant until the property is paid for, so you also have a say in how the property is maintained. But there is a high incentive for that individual to take very good care of this property.

## Listen to What Other Wealthy People are Doing

The key to creating extreme wealth is to build passive income streams. Some of the ideas here may resonate with you, some may not. One of the best ways to find, create and benefit from passive income streams is to start listening to what your wealthy friends are doing and create the same kinds of income streams for yourself. There are literally thousands of passive income streams available for anyone to create immediately. All you have to do is start hunting for them.

## EXERCISES

1.  Identify some events in your life that have brought money into your life.

2.  Identify income streams that have brought money into your life.

3.  Identify your current most productive linear income streams. How can you improve these income streams? If these are associated with your job, how can you be more effective with your use of time? Tim Ferris, in his book *The 4-Hour Workweek*, made an excellent suggestion when he observed the trend in business of allowing employees to work from home. You may want to consider a discussion with your employer on how your time can be used more effectively. Remember, productivity isn't just getting paid more, it can also involve decreasing the commitment of hours spent.

4.  A first step in becoming more productive in a linear income stream is to become aware of what activities are generating the best results. (Remember the 80/20 rule.) When you can identify which activities are providing the greatest returns, then you can explore how you can do more of those activities. If you are involved in a job as your linear income stream, discuss with your employer what activities they feel are of the most value and determine how more of those activities can be done. Suggest a compensation structure that rewards you for increased productivity.

5.  Identify passive income streams currently providing contributions to your finances. Are these based on your business or the efforts of others? If they are based on your business, how can you improve these systems?

6.  What systems exist around you that are worthwhile investments for you? Will these create passive income streams?

What is required of you to participate? Keep in mind that the rewards may be different. Some will create cash flow while others are assets. Some will be both. Determine whether the systems you've chosen create cash flow or are assets. Is this what you want?

7. Set up a system so that your passive income returns can reinvest in themselves automatically.

8. Regularly monitor your passive income streams and be on the lookout for bigger and better. When a passive income stream stops performing, requires more of your time and effort or a better opportunity comes along, carefully consider shifting to that new opportunity. Wealth is created by always looking for better and better opportunities.

9. At the conclusion of this chapter I shared two strategies that I have used to create passive income streams, namely loans and rent-to-own real estate. As you have probably recognized, these models require resourcefulness and creativity to construct. What are some creative ways that you may be able to innovate on current money-making strategies? How can you make them accessible to you right now?

10. Get to work and create a new passive income stream this week. It doesn't have to return a lot of money. Just create it so you can experience what it's like to start receiving a flow of funds to you without having to babysit the experience.

## QUESTIONS

1. How is money currently arriving in your life?
2. What are the most common events in your life that have brought money to you?
3. How can you create more of those events?
4. How can you facilitate the addition of new events in your life?
5. What are the current linear income streams in your life right now?

6.  What would you need to accomplish financially to replace your job as a linear income stream?
7.  What passive income streams are you currently benefiting from?
8.  What systems have others created that you can take advantage of through investment?
9.  How are you using the returns from your income streams?
10. What other passive income opportunities are around you?
11. Is your money operating in the best systems available to you?
12. Are your income streams becoming a babysitting job and requiring too much time?
13. Are you evaluating your income streams by logic or emotion?
14. Are there better opportunities for you to shift your efforts and resources to than the ones you are currently engaged in?

# Millionaires and Strategy

**THERE IT WAS.** The headline of the morning business paper. "Millionaires on the rise." It almost sounded like the title of a horror film. *"Oh no! The millionaires are coming and no one can stop them!"* Just like in a horror movie, whatever the millionaires touch will become infected, or rather, affected. When we recognize the effect that millionaires have in our environment I call this the millionaire effect.

When you consider the effect that millionaires have on the world around them, it is incredible. Here are a few easy-to-view effects that are in plain view. Millionaires:

- affect the quality of life for themselves and others around them
- contribute to their communities
- create systems and tools that make life easier for many.
- inspire others to reach a greater potential.
- affect generations to come, not only in their own families, but throughout the world
- generally target their ideas outward for the world to use
- have a positive effect on the global economy

Millionaires understand that abundance requires them to be involved and of benefit to others to be most effective.

While there are literally a million ways to create a million dollars, I would like to share three very straightforward places to make money. I can only talk about what I know and I will only talk about what I have been successful with. Now, while what I am about to share doesn't guarantee success, I have found that these ideas have been very effective for growing wealth for me quickly.

## IT'S TIME TO GET PERSONAL

As we near the end of this book, I want to consolidate some of the lessons I've shared and relate a few examples and thoughts from my own life experience to help you be successful. As part of these lessons I want to share a few things from my own portfolio.

Before I share these things, I want to emphasize that I do not think one of these areas is better than another. In fact, many times they overlap. I'll explain a little bit more about what I mean by that in a minute. I participate in each of these areas and they are all effective in different ways. I share them with you for you to consider in your r pursuit of wealth.

### Investments and Business

Before I get too far into explaining about specific categories of investment and business, I want to clearly state that I believe that everything is an investment and everything is a business.

Whether you are buying or starting a business, purchasing real estate or forming the relationships that we will speak about later, it is all an investment and all a business.

In this category, I want to address what is typically thought of when people talk about investing. The traditional view of investing involves utilizing your money by investing in a third-party offering. As the discussion continues, you'll notice that I omit bank products, mutual funds, stocks and bonds, and many of the traditional financial instruments. It's not that I don't think they are useful. I have seen a lot of people create highly secure and financially effective portfolios with those kinds of things. Some people swear by them, and I have those things in my portfolio too. I just haven't built or continued to exponentially grow my wealth with them. As a result they did not make the list in Guerrilla Millionaire strategies.

Traditional investment instruments are built for consistent, secure and steady savings in growth portfolios, and to become a millionaire with them can often take years. The investments I want to share in this section can do the same in a fraction of the time.

Now as I said a moment ago, everything is a business. As a business owner, you will be required to inject time, effort and capital to keep things running smoothly. If it's done right, you may be able to build this business so that it becomes passive and your time commitment and effort become minimal.

Now is a good time to share my definition of productivity. Too many people think that productivity is finding a way to do more so that you can get more. I find that productivity is rather a determination to do less and get more. Or to have what you do create more impact on the activities around you. Things in my business generally run better when I get out of the way and create a system that works without me. I encourage you to do the same.

### Everything is Negotiable

Now, before I share these investment possibilities an important point that applies to all of the strategies in this section, whether they have to do with investment, business, real estate or even how money is made in relationships is negotiation. Although at first glance it may appear pretty evident, you'd be surprised how many people neglect to implement this strategy into their wealth-growing arsenal. This little key is worth millions on its own. The key is to remember that everything is negotiable.

If someone wants access to your money or you are investing your money, you are the one who holds the power. You can negotiate more favorable terms. You don't have to get involved in a cookie-cutter agreement.

As you negotiate, you can tip concessions in your favor and position yourself for incredible future benefits. So before you engage in anything, ask this question before signing anything or giving a dime of your money: "Is that the best you can do?"

You'd be surprised at the difference a few percentage points, the restructuring of a time frame or the addition of a security clause can make to protect and grow your interests. And if there is one thing that I've learned it's that if the person offering you the opportunity is unwilling to bend, you can always find another deal down the road that will be open to exploring possibilities. This is especially true in the bigger deals. The bigger the deal, the more room there is for negotiation.

Negotiation was something that I learned early on in my wealth-building career from my mentors. At first I was a little nervous to try it out. But here's how that went.

One of the first investments I made was in a commercial real estate venture. A company in my hometown operated a trust fund that was used to acquire existing commercial buildings, give them a face-lift and then either put them back on the market or fill them with tenants. The offering was a 10% annual return paid out in cash dividends every month and then, at the conclusion of four years, a return of the entire principal. In my eyes as a novice investor, this was a pretty good deal. I was ready to get involved with those terms without question. But I remembered the words of my mentors to always negotiate.

In fact, one of them specifically gave me this simple technique, and I have used it often with great success. The technique is very straightforward. Once the person you are negotiating with presents their offer, even if you like it, ask, "Is that the best you can do?" and then stop talking.

I decided to try this technique with this company. I asked the question and then I paused. Without any resistance the company altered the agreement to give me a 12% annual return and an additional 10% on my money at the conclusion of the four years.

The funny thing about this story is that I didn't expect to receive anything. I was ready to accept the deal as it was. Even when I asked, "Is that the best you can do?" I didn't expect to change the deal, but they were happy to accommodate. Now here I am, several years later, and I still invest with this group, and we always negotiate every investment and everyone wins.

## Business

I recently read that of all the self-made millionaires created in the world today, 84% started or own their business. If that many self-made millionaires are made in this category, it definitely merits a closer look. Here are a few options.

### Starting or Buying a Business

You may have a great idea for a business. Keep in mind that not all businesses are winners. A lot of businesses fail, and the vast majority of businesses make under $200 thousand a year. That's quite a distance from a million.

But I love business. I like to start businesses and I also like to buy them. Buying them is often a very good way to avoid start-up risks and headaches. Buying a business is kind of like buying real estate. You look for something you like. You look for something that has the potential to make money for you. You look for something that is priced below what it is worth. You can then hang on to it as an income source or sell it for a profit after making a few improvements.

Here are a few quick questions that I consider when building a business and ask when I am looking at buying a business:

- What's my gut feeling about this business?
- Is this business something that interests me?
- Does it have a strong client base?
- Is there a continuing interested audience ready to pay for this product or service?

- Is there an effective system to make this transaction or if not, how easily can one be created?
- Is there management in place to keep the system running or improve upon it?
- Does this business model have the potential for growth?

The answers to those questions dictate whether or not I will move forward. If you aren't making money, you won't have the privilege of being in business long, and it certainly won't help you to reach your goal of becoming a millionaire.

While there is a sense of satisfaction in starting your own business, you can spend a lot of money doing so. It is always easier and generally more productive to buy an existing business with all of the systems and tools in place. This approach generally allows you to begin with cash flow in place.

## A Little More on Buying Businesses

There are lots of great business to buy. Buying a business is a much easier and safer bet in my opinion. Statistics confirm that the majority of new businesses fail in the first two years. The majority of businesses are not profitable in their first five years. And then there are the issues of building your brand, finding customers and systematizing all of the details to be able to serve them. Why wouldn't you just select a business that already has all these things in place and a proven track record, and start there? It makes a lot more sense, is far more profitable and costs you less in the end.

You'd be surprised at the way these deals can be structured. You never know why someone is looking to sell their business.

In my quest for opportunities I found a wellness center that had been operating for nearly two decades. They had a large and loyal clientele, and the revenue stream seemed consistent. After answering "yes" to all of the above questions, I decided to meet with the owner of the company.

The company was owned by an older couple who had decided it

was time to retire. However, I could sense that while they were interested in the financial benefits of selling the business, the husband wasn't entirely keen on stepping totally out of the picture. So we structured things differently than a straight-out sale, and instead of me becoming the owner, I became a partner.

The husband continued to work with the new management team part-time, as often as he wanted to. I established another passive income stream for myself without having to put in any time or effort at all.

In our agreement, I positioned myself so that when my new partners grew weary of the business, I would have first right of refusal to buy the rest of the company. I have built many deals where the original owners and I have become partners. Sometimes we have used the existing management, and other times we have completely restructured the venture. Remember that everything is negotiable, and you don't always have to buy the entire company.

There are many brokers and organizations that sell businesses. You can find many of them online. I like using brokerages when buying businesses, because most of the time they have done much of your sifting already. They generally won't list a business unless they believe they can sell it, which means they have already explored the financials, legal documents and assets to ensure that everything they are representing is true.

Naturally, you will want to do your due diligence as well, but generally speaking, brokerages give you a pretty fair head start. It's like using a real estate agent when buying real estate. And by the way, brokerages generally charge the seller their fee, not you.

### Selling a Business

While I like to buy businesses and hold on to them for cash flow or an increase in value, I also like to sell businesses. Sometimes you can make a lot of money doing this. Think of it like buying a fixer-upper in real estate. You see a business that has potential, but maybe it is not quite running at maximum performance. (Businesses being sold by people retiring are a great example. Perhaps the owners have become stale in how they have things systematized or are not even aware of new technology that could automate things for them, allowing for more income.)

Often when I see an opportunity like this, I will buy the company, give it a face-lift, increase the numbers and then go hunting for a new buyer. Buying and selling businesses is a great strategy for growing wealth.

### Real Estate

I separated real estate from the investment category above. Some people may agree with me, others may not. There are two reasons I have separated real estate from investment.

First, real estate is an investment, but only if it is making you money. Often, with fluctuations in the market, it is an asset, but it can often be a liability too. In some cases, a property yields positive cash flow, but we live in an imperfect world. Sometimes the property is not making money, especially if it's vacant.

Second, the investments listed above are generally passive income streams. Remember that passive means you don't have to get involved. Real estate can often be more hands-on unless you have a management company supporting you, or in the case of commercial real estate investing, you are an investor or part owner sharing or delegating the management of the property to a third party.

### Residential

Residential real estate is likely the most popularly discussed method of creating additional income. The typical model is to buy a property and rent it out, making money from the rent payments of the tenants and also receiving the benefit of the property value increasing over time. The second most common approach is to buy a property, fix it up and then sell it. This is commonly known as a flip. But just as there are many creative ways to negotiate in business deals, there are also many strategies and options to consider with making money in real estate. I'll just share one that is among my favorites.

## Rent to Own

I talked about this a little in the previous chapter, but I want to go into more detail here. Rather than simply rent a property I like to offer a rent-to-own opportunity to my tenants. The reason why is simple.

If you have a stake in ownership of the property you live in, you take care of it better. This approach also eliminates the hassle of having to hire and pay a management company. Naturally, with rent to own the tenant is paying a premium for this opportunity, and you come out financially ahead.

Let me share a recent example. Currently the real estate market in certain parts of the United States has taken quite a dip, especially markets like Nevada and Arizona.

In fact, I have found several condominium properties in Las Vegas that, prior to this current recession, were valued at over $250 thousand and are now going for as little as $40 thousand.

The only problem for most people is that they have to pay for the property in full. They can't finance a penny of it.

Naturally, there are people eager to take advantage of this current dip in the market. They know that in the near future things will change, and it is very likely that the value of that condo will return to somewhere in the mid-$200 thousand range.

So here are the basics of what I do: I buy the condo for $40 thousand and I do a rent-to-own deal with my new tenant. I agree to sell the property back to them over a certain period of time at the price of $150 thousand or so, and I act as their bank, so there will be interest and other associated fees charged on that transaction. Essentially, it's the same as a traditional mortgage.

The tenant wins because now they get into a property that is priced below where they hope the market will be in five years, and all the way they are building equity. I win because over the next five years, my $40 thousand investment turns into $160 thousand, giving me a profit of $120 thousand.

And by the way, the entire time my name is on the title for security, and if the tenant defaults on payments, I have written into my agreement that they forfeit all past payments as equity in the property. It simply becomes as though they had been a renter. Isn't this similar to what the banks do?

## Commercial Real Estate

A quick note on my experience in commercial real estate. I like commercial real estate, especially when there is a management company in place to handle the asset. I find that commercial tenants are less needy overall than residential tenants, and there are fewer challenges collecting the rent. Again, this is speaking strictly from my own experience.

Even better than owning the property outright is the fact that in commercial real estate, it's more interesting to find potential partners. I have several commercial real estate assets where I am a partner, and it becomes easier to mitigate risk and minimize the amount of capital I have to part with.

## Relationships

You may think it odd to list relationships alongside investments, business, and real estate as a money-making tool. But I assure you this is no accident. Relationships are among the most profitable tools you can use to grow your wealth.

## Getting Dialed in

In business, there are two categories of relationship: informal or formal. Formal relationships are when you know someone from a distance. You know what they do, you've got their card and when you bump into them at social functions you have a pleasant interaction.

Very little business happens in these more formal relationships. However, the informal relationships are another matter.

I have made a lot of money from informal relationships, and I have helped a lot of other people make money in these kinds of informal relationships. These informal relationships are people who become my friends and advisors. It is in this area that I hear about and find some of the best opportunities for wealth growth and support. The truth of the matter is that by the time the public in general hears about an opportunity it is gone. That's why you need your friends to share information as it happens. It's just like a news report. The breaking news is always the best because you can respond.

### Become a Connector

Becoming a connector of people can be a very profitable source of wealth. One of my favorite experiences of how being a connector paid off occurred in the following experience.

This is what happened. I have always known that money could be made by simply connecting people who needed money with people who had money. So I began to get the word out that I was a connector. The idea took off almost instantly and made me quite a bit of money, as you will see. It was really quite simple.

What I did was I met with several people who had money, and structured an agreement whereby I would be paid a 20% finder's fee for any exciting and potentially profitable investment opportunities I brought them. Naturally, they would have to approve the opportunity, but if they did, they would pay me 20% of whatever was funded.

I then went and found opportunities that needed money and fit the criteria my money sources were looking for. With this group seeking money I structured an agreement that would pay me 20% of whatever money I could steer their way.

Once I had these agreements in place I would then make the introduction between these people and the rest is history.

The most that I ever made for one single introduction was $400 thousand, and the entire process took me about three hours. Now, these kinds of deals are not always that easy. But that was my favorite one.

## Solving Problems for those in Your Network

The value which you receive will be in proportion to the problems which you are able to solve. It only makes sense then that the larger the problem you solve, the more of a reward you can expect. Look for the biggest problems that you can provide solutions for and you will soon find that you are very valuable to those in your network.

---

### LESSONS FROM EXPERIENCE

1. Before becoming involved in a business, consider whether the business has the ability to solve problems for people in the long term. Businesses that are based on a fad or a temporary need should be sold quickly as possible once they're up and running.

    Make a list of the kinds of businesses you would be interested in buying before you go shopping. And naturally, before you buy anything, be sure to compare pricing so that you have a clear view of what the market value is for specific business models and locations.

2. Never pay what is being asked. Always negotiate. Simply ask the question, "Is that the best you can do?" each time someone presents you with an opportunity. The key to having this work effectively is to ask the question and then stop talking and listen. It's that simple.

3. How often are you connecting with the relationships that will bring you the greatest value in your wealth-building efforts? What are you doing to nurture these relationships? What do you really want from these relationships, and how are you communicating those objectives with clarity and specificity?

---

4. Consider the people currently in your contact list and think about who among them could be put together for a benefit. Meet with each party and ask them what such an introduction might be worth to them. Structure a deal so that you will be compensated for those introductions, and collect on the value you have created.

## QUESTIONS

1. Why is everything an investment?
2. What can you negotiate on any given opportunity to make it more favorable for you?
3. When looking at an opportunity to lend money, what is the security?
4. Have you put strong terms and penalties in place?
5. What are your collection processes in money lending?
6. Does your investment provide regular cash flow?
7. What are the key considerations when starting a business or buying one?
8. What is your exit strategy for your business?
9. If you are involved in real estate rental properties, how are they currently managed?
10. What relationships do you currently have that could contribute to your wealth-building goals?
11. What relationships can you nurture that could help you achieve your financial goals?
12. What informal relationships are you currently involved in that might be helpful to you?
13. Who in your network should meet? How can you benefit from the introduction?
14. What problems are you able to provide solutions for?

# Getting Started on Your First Million

## THE IMPORTANT FIRST STEPS

**YIKES!** I could feel myself cringing inside as my son overturned the key to the ignition in the car. That violent, eardrum-shattering screech is a sure indicator of a new driver nearby. I've made that sound and most likely you have, too.

But this time it was personal. My fourteen-year-old son, Jared, was learning how to drive. Learning how to drive is an event that many people in North America experience. The majority of people who face this challenge generally do so in their mid-teens, but some people face it later in life. This challenge fills many people with fear, others with excitement and anticipation. My daughter was one of the excited ones and still loves to drive. That excitement will probably never die for her. And now my son is looking forward to driving because he knows that greater freedom and opportunity are ahead.

Now how does this relate to making money, wealth and, specifically, becoming a Guerrilla Millionaire? There are a lot of similarities, actually. Let me share my experience and explain how the two subjects are related.

For me, getting my driver's license at sixteen was like embarking on a new adventure. I knew that a lot of freedom and opportunity came with that privilege. But because I was on the verge of something new it was also scary.

I remember when I was around twelve my dad asked me if I wanted to back the car out of the driveway. I was excited to try, but I was also terrified. I remember him giving me his keys and climbing into the passenger seat beside me.

To be honest, I wasn't even sure how to start the car. But I tried and made that huge, terrible screeching noise as I overturned the key. The car roared as I put my foot straight down hard on the gas pedal. It was a good thing it wasn't in gear.

If my dad had second thoughts about letting me drive, he didn't express them. Instead he paused, gave me some clear instructions, corrected a few of my misconceptions and let me try again.

The second time was much better. My confidence went up. He then talked me through how to put the car in reverse and then to slowly (he stressed *slowly*) take my foot off the brake and then gently (he also stressed *gently*) place my foot (he stressed *gently* again) on the gas pedal.

Naturally, my first touch to the gas pedal gave us a little bump as the car bolted into action. Quickly I shifted my foot hard to the brake. My dad laughed as I jolted him forward and back in his seat. (I later experienced exactly the same thing when I taught Jared how to drive. I guess it must be something that every generation experiences.)

My self-confidence teetered again, back to the unsure side of things. Once again my dad told me to relax and reminded me of what to do. My confidence hadn't fully returned, but I had more confidence than fear so I tried again. This time things went much more smoothly.

From that experience I continued to learn more and more about driving, and when the day finally came for me to take the driver's test, I passed. (Actually, the *second* time I took the test I passed.)

So here are the similarities between learning to drive and wealth building.

## Discomfort and Fear

When most people set out on a mission to create more abundance in their lives, they are quite excited. There can be quite a bit of fear and discomfort, too. The first element of this fear comes from not knowing how to start. Many people are just like me when my dad gave me the keys. I didn't even know how to get things started.

This fear and discomfort comes not only from a lack of knowledge, but also from believing that if things go wrong, they could go horribly wrong. In wealth building, people fear that if things go horribly wrong they might lose all the money they had to start with. It has been my experience that this fear of losing money is often more powerful than any hope of reward. Because this fear is more powerful than the reward, people become paralyzed and do nothing. This fear keeps a lot of people from starting down the path to becoming a millionaire and changing their life.

*Discomfort is the first step toward great success.*

## You May not Begin Smoothly

Having correct expectations can really make a significant difference when it comes to growing wealth. There will be bumps along the way, and not everything will always go smoothly. In my pursuit of learning and teaching about this subject, I have conducted extensive research into the lives of more than 400 of the world's top achievers. Many of the people involved in this research were highly wealthy individuals. If there was one common denominator amongst the top achievers I researched, it was that everyone experienced ups and downs in their journey to create abundance.

*If something is worth doing well, it is worth doing poorly at first.*
—Brian Tracy

## It doesn't Take a Lot to Get the Car Moving

When I gently touched the gas pedal, the car started to move. This is also true of your financial success. It doesn't take a big action to create a huge effect on long-term results. Wealth is easier to build through consistency than through large one-time actions.

Most people believe that they need to have a huge amount of money before they can make an impact on their immediate finances. The truth is that all big results start as little efforts. As soon as you understand the impact that your smallest actions have on creating big future results, the sooner you will reach financial freedom.

*The Great Wall of China is the world's biggest man-made object, but upon closer examination, it is simply a structure built of small bricks.*

## The importance of a mentor

As I sat in the driver's seat, my father was a huge support to me. It is always difficult to attempt something new. And even harder if you have to attempt that new thing without help or support.

Real wealth is grown with the support of mentors because you can only rise as high as what you understand you should do. If you don't know what steps to take toward your goal, you can't start walking in that direction.

*Better is one day with a great teacher than a hundred years of experience alone.*
—Japanese proverb

Finding a mentor often isn't enough. There are a lot of good potential mentors out there, but many of them are either too busy to teach or are not skilled as teachers. You should always be on the lookout for good teachers, and when the opportunity to study with one comes, take advantage of it.

## You Get Better as You Continue

Practice makes perfect, and as you get better you develop competence and confidence. I remember how nervous I was backing out of that driveway so long ago and compare it to how I feel about driving now. I have no nervousness at all. In fact, sometimes (and I'm sure you have done it too) I can eat, talk on the phone or even change a CD while driving. While I encourage you to keep your eyes on the road, I want to point out that you and I may start off as nervous drivers, but soon we have all kinds of confidence and can perform almost any task required of us in the car with ease. The same is true with wealth building. As you gain more experience in building your wealth, it won't be long until you are able to go forward with confidence and even expand the basic abilities required.

## A Note about Cruise Control

Sticking with the driving analogy, I still remember the first time I discovered cruise control. Naturally, I was already driving and had quite a bit of experience on the road by the time I really understood what cruise control was for. But there it was. It allowed to me to put my driving efforts almost on autopilot. The same will happen as you build your wealth-building skills. Soon your money-making machine will be on autopilot, and all you will have to do is steer.

## Freedom and Opportunity Expands

The biggest thing that I remember my high school driving instructor saying is that with the privilege of driving comes much more freedom and opportunity. This idea is very connected with wealth building as well. If you use your wealth to create and expand the best things in your life, you will find your freedom and opportunities will also expand. Ultimately your reward is in passing it on.

Like my dad taught me to drive, I taught my son and daughter how to drive, and most likely they will pass these lessons on to their children and so on and so on. While I still enjoy the experience of driving, I also find a lot of joy in seeing my children with this same freedom. (Not to mention how much freedom has come to me because I no longer have to drive them around or pick them up.)

The same can be said of wealth. When you have the skills to change your own life and then are able to pass those same skills along to another, there is a satisfaction and joy that comes to you. And as I did with my children, you will empower others to solve their own challenges and accomplish the goals which they have for themselves. There isn't a much greater feeling than that.

### Are You Ready to Go?

Before you get the car rolling there are a few things that you have to have in place.

The first is the car keys. I think that in wealth, the key could really be compared to your financial goal and then to the right attitude, the desire and the belief in yourself to achieve that goal. When you have a clear view of what you want and a commitment to get it, you have the key to get started.

The next thing you need is a seat belt. I think a seat belt could be compared to having consistency in action. While consistency is something you can regulate yourself, I still feel the best way to build consistency into your plan in this day and age is to automate your wealth processes. In other words, use the technology in the banking world to build automatic money transfers to feed your investments and your opportunities. Seat belts keep you safe in the midst of chaos. Real life can be chaotic, so if you can build mechanisms like electronic fund transfers to do a good portion of the work for you, your financial future will be easier to attain.

## EXERCISES

Think about everything you have learned in this book. What is the most important thing you have learned based on your current situation, and how will that lesson make your life better? How can you implement that lesson to have the most impact in your life right now?

## QUESTIONS

The most important question of this book:

What will you do now?

# About the Authors

## JAY CONRAD LEVINSON
## (CREATOR OF THE GUERRILLA SERIES)

Jay Levinson, known everywhere as "the Father of Guerrilla Marketing," may be the most noted marketing man in the world. His 58-plus books have sold over 20 million copies and now appear in 62 languages worldwide. They're required reading in many MBA programs around the world. He was born in Detroit, raised in Chicago and graduated from the University of Colorado. His studies in psychology led him to advertising agencies, including a directorship at Leo Burnett in London, where he served as creative director.

A winner of many media awards, he has been part of the creative teams that made household names of the Marlboro Man, the Pillsbury Dough Boy, Allstate's Good Hands, United's Friendly Skies, the Sears DieHard battery, Tony the Tiger and the Jolly Green Giant.

Today the Guerrilla brand is one of the most powerful brands in the history of marketing and business.

Want to hire Jay to speak at your event? Go to www.gmarketing.com or www.Guerrillamarketingassociation.com.

## DOUGLAS VERMEEREN
## (AUTHOR OF *GUERRILLA MILLIONAIRE*)

Douglas Vermeeren is the CEO of Millionaire Training Systems which shares strategies that everyday people can use to create amazing wealth in their lives. He grows his wealth through investment, real estate, money lending, buying and selling businesses and building relationships.

Early in his career he conducted extensive research into the lives of more than 400 of the world's top achievers. This is similar to the study that Napoleon Hill conducted for his book *Think and Grow Rich*. It is for this reason that many refer to Douglas Vermeeren as the modern-day Napoleon Hill.

Vermeeren's findings on success have been published in many books, with a focus on finance, wealth and achievement. Currently his books are available in 22 languages around the world.

He is the creator of the hit personal-development films *The Opus* and *The Gratitude Experiment* and The Treasure Map.

In 2011, Doug Vermeeren was nominated as one of the top public speakers in the world by the Association of Professional Coaches, Trainers and Consultants.

Want to hire Doug to speak at your next event?

Call 1-877-393-9496 or go to www.DouglasVermeeren.com

You can find more about Millionaire Training Systems and the programs available to you by going to www.MillionaireTrainingSystems.com

Printed in the United States
By Bookmasters